SOUL
EXPERIENCE

SOUL
EXPERIENCE

THE 4TH LEVEL OF IDENTITY

AL KILLEEN

I M P

Denver, Colorado

SOUL EXPERIENCE: THE 4TH LEVEL OF IDENTITY

All Internet addresses (websites, blogs, etc.) noted in this book are used as a resource. They are operated by their respective owners, and the mention herein does not in any way imply an endorsement by the author or publisher.

Disclaimer: The following information is offered purely as insight from my personal life journey and the journeys of countless others whom I have had the honor of sharing my life path with and supported as a friend, family member, and professional business/life coach. It is not intended as a medical, psychological, or professional replacement for your particular needs along your path. If you are utilizing medical or psychological support from a professional medical resource, please defer to that resource before implementing any of the following ideas or activities.

Requests for information should be addressed to
Integrative Mastery Programs
killeen@conciergemarketing.com
www.IntegrativeMasteryPrograms.com

Paperback ISBN: 978-1-947547-01-8
Mobi ISBN: 978-1-947547-02-5
EPUB ISBN: 978-1-947547-03-2
Audio ISBN: 978-1-947547-04-9

Library of Congress Cataloguing-in-Publication Data on file with the publisher.
LCCN: 2018930152

Production and publishing: Concierge Marketing Inc. www.conciergemarketing.com

Printed in the United States of America

10 9 8 7 6 5 4 3 2 1

This book is dedicated to all those brave Souls throughout history that have experienced the sufferings of life while courageously endeavoring to understand, trust and love it nonetheless. Those are the Light Workers who have revealed that we are not just our physical selves, but rather forces within the Tao who have been gifted with Consciousness to interpret life at a deeper level—the level of the Source. They have proven that we all have Buddha Nature... Christ Consciousness... Enlightenment within us, if we simply seek it through the messages of the Avatars who have come and gone amidst us and guided those seeking to understand the true nature of human existence. And beyond seeking it, we must subsequently Be those messages of hope, love and faith that guide us to the true understanding of our eternal nature within our temporal one.

Accordingly, this book is dedicated to the Human Spirit that is, in the end, Divine Spirit once understood in its true form.

"The Tao that can be named... is not the Tao."

To acknowledge some is to leave out others, and who along my path of life has not contributed to the information in this book? God? My beloved wife and sons? My dearest friends? My dear clients? Even my challengers and obstructionists along the way?

Who?

None. You have all made this happen, in one way or another. This book acknowledges all those emissaries of Divinity along the way who have guided me to the beginning point of understanding... even those who didn't know they were.

TESTIMONIALS & ENDORSEMENTS

I don't know about you, but I am always a bit guarded when I come across some book that promises to change my life. I've been disappointed too many times to believe them anymore… at least based on the proclamations of the author or the superstar names he or she might have paid to endorse the material within the book. I'm not saying that it is disingenuous, but rather feels a bit manipulative… to me at least.

Accordingly, I sent an invitation to some of my clients, friends and colleagues (actually, my life-Brothers and life-Sisters), and the following is what they sent back. They have been left in original form, with the only edits being for typographical errors or to embolden any insights that seemed particularly important for potential readers.

These are people from all walks of life, all levels of the socio-economic spectrum—from CEOs to Homemakers and everything in between. Various genders, races, ages and walks of life. May these, your peers in this life at this time on the planet, offer their experiences about what the information in this book may do for you if you read and follow it.

You are welcome to skip this chapter if you don't want to see how the outcome could be for you if you value what others have done with their "Level 4" Identity… but it may be quite helpful in opening your mind to what will be a life-transforming journey if you wish to take it.

My life has been enriched and blessed by practicing my Level 4 and exposure to the concepts of Integrative Mastery. I have embraced the program with a loving and open heart. My family and work relationships are more fulfilled, and I am dedicated to living my life in Level 4. If you are at a crossroad in your life and feel that this is all there is, take a walk with Al, you will not regret it. **Integrative Mastery and coming to understand and practice my Level 4 saved my life.** *I thought I was doing great and living my life at the utmost. Little did I know, I was a wreck! Inside and outside, I was a mess. My first exposure to Integrative Mastery had me in tears. Tears of joy, tears of happiness and tears of hope. Thank you for your vision and helping me know that there is a higher level of living. Thank you, Al Killeen!*

—Debbie Havens
Mortgage Lender/Manager/Wife

Having recently completed my Integrative Mastery Program with Al **I have great optimism in transforming my personal and professional life from the unfulfilled and ungrateful feelings from the conditioned Level 3 ways I knew to the joyful and rewarding soul I know I will possess from living a Level 4 life.** *Thank you Al for energizing my Faith and enriching my life.*

—Craig Fleming
Father/Husband/Business Owner

*Being made aware of Level 4 living has shifted the lens of my life perspective. Level 4 is a wonderful label to put on something all of us have within. It is a reminder, a call to be the best version of ourselves, not for notoriety, but for feeding our soul, and being able to be very aware of all that is going on around us. We are all here on this journey of life to learn and to grow. **Being aware of Level 4, and taking on each day from that space, that perspective, will make all the difference in how we live out each day in this thing we call life, and will bring a satisfaction that will long surpass this existence.***

—Jared Peterson
Father/Business Owner/Light Worker

While I continue to learn and practice every day how to "be" my best "Level 4" Self, the experience of truly focusing on it has changed my life for the better in so many ways, but particularly in my relationships with other people which are much more positive and rewarding than before.

My Level 4 Self has allowed me to be a more understanding Christian; a more loving husband to my bride of 44 years; a more inspirational father and grandfather; and a more insightful and patient leader, coach, and manager *in my chosen profession of Mortgage banking.*

Thank you Al, for helping me be a Better ME!!!

—Gene Humphries
Husband/Father/Grandfather/
Division/President/Believer

Testimonials continued on page 227

CONTENTS

PREFACE

This book is about you. You may not know it yet, but it is. It's also about me and the woman over on the corner across the street, and the guy who just drove by, perhaps a little too fast for a crowded street, and is now out of sight.

Being human is really challenging; it's hard work. The payoff is a life well-lived. But what, exactly, does that mean?

For many, if not most, it means to become better and better at who you are when you leave your parental home. Perhaps that is the reason that for longer than we all care to acknowledge, we believe, because we were taught to believe this way, that we all were fully formed by an early age and thereafter we just got older and perfected that early Self. The cartoon character Popeye said it best of all, "I yam who I yam." Nice defense for most situations. Truth be told, we have all used it to wiggle out of tight spots. "I couldn't help myself, dad, I am who I am."

Or we didn't buy into that world view, and struck out on an adventure to make ourselves something or someone that we wanted to be despite it all. Either way, the notion that there was much beyond those early years, more stages of a human life, to engage—well, that was not even something to contemplate, or if you did set out to challenge it, to have a nagging doubt that maybe all your efforts to prove otherwise were doomed to futility and failure.

Freud was perhaps the avatar of the notion that "the prologue is the rest, too." Then there was Jung, and the hopeful concept that we are always adapting ourselves to new possibilities—indeed, we cannot resist being the principal adaptors in our own lives—gained a small but growing audience.

With adaptation comes higher levels of self-awareness and self-understanding.

Along for the ride as well is a higher level of scariness. No wonder children resist changing from the comfort of being themselves as they are today, or at least as they perceive themselves to be. Without the notion of a long future and with no overview interpretation of their short past, perhaps we cannot expect much more from them.

But we adults can do better even if we are disinclined to admit it to others, least of all our parental units.

I remember the times in my life when my parents would query "when are you going to grow up? Find yourself. Become a man. Do this that or the other thing and make something of your life. Be a better version of the person you became under our guidance."

You have your story—your version of that experience.

Meanwhile, life happens. It's more of a shared experience than we are oft willing to admit. Even to ourselves. We vector our way across it and the cumulative effect of many small adjustments in direction lead to powerful impacts on who we become. Little changes accumulate. Time is an ally of all this and time guarantees that we can never be a mere extension of exactly that person our parents launched as young adults into the world.

I remember as a child thinking "will I ever grow up?" Today, in retirement, with children and grandchildren and even great grandchildren to come who are now twinkles in their parent's eyes (I can see them), I hope and pray that I never will "grow up." Growing up and growing older are not the same. I'll spare you the essay here on why. You could write it yourself.

I do know that despite the continuous process of change and evolution in defining who I am, I still am not limitless in my prospects for the future. Biology will kick in soon enough and call a halt to it all. But until then, I press on.

Al Killeen taught me that the early levels of identity in this developmental process are both powerful as you live through them and insufficient for your life's fullness in the future. The Fourth Level of Identity compels you to ask, again and again, who am I and how can I make that state of becoming my best Self be important both to me and especially to others?

Put another way, if you are that one grain of sand on the beach, then life as you know it might be terrific. But if you, as that grain of sand, embark upon an involuntary adventure (and who hasn't?) then the adjective "terrific" not only opens up the possibilities of being the ultimate grain of sand on that or some other beach; it super charges the meaning of yourself in both your own life and in the lives of everyone else you encounter.

Your uniqueness and the power of your being both acted upon and an actor in the drama of life shapes who you are and how you express that experience to the world—to those around you.

But here is the key. You cannot just have the experiences, wonderful as they might be. Nothing wrong with that, of course, and if as a result you can develop an awareness of their meaning to you in your life, so much the better.

But imagine the power of being aware of the experiences, being transformed by them, engaging them and then consciously picking up your own grains of sand as you move along through life and taking those grains with you as beneficiaries of your journey and of their own as well.

To do that is to be in Killeen's Fourth Level of Identity and the power of that life is not fully describable to others. Read the book, however, and you cannot fail to describe it for yourself. Therein lies its power for you, me and countless others.

—Charles R. Middleton
The Author's College Mentor (1971-1975)
President Emeritus, Roosevelt University

FOREWORD

Trillions. The number of cells in the human body. Trillions. The number of gallons of water in the Earth's ocean in a cubic mile. Trillions. The number of galaxies in the Universe. Trillions. The number of grains of sand on the beaches of the world. One. You.

In a timeless and ancient story, a fable is told of the *Origin of Love and Hope*. As the story goes, on a beautiful sunlit beach, a single black grain of sand was contemplating its good fortune. How lucky it was to live on this gorgeous, sunny beach, being washed and massaged each day by the turquoise tides. It was gently caressed day in and day out… for eons. It was pushed and pulled, rolled and shifted, rolled and pulled, shifted and pushed. It had once been part of the original molten black lava that flowed from deep under the sea floor. The lava layered upon itself again and again for millions of years, until one day, this lava of volcanic origin broke through the surface of the sea, and slowly became an island.

For millennia, the storms would sweep their mighty crests of foam and spray over the lava formations, and slowly, very slowly, the lava began a transformation… a metamorphosis. It was changing shape, texture, size, and form. Finely textured grains of beautiful black sand were being created. Over time, this island begat life… first as bacteria and microorganisms, later as seeds and spores. Then birds and other lifeforms slowly found their way to this tiny isle. It was no longer a molten flow of hot lava which built upon itself layer by layer. No, it was now a beautiful beach of endless black sand. A trillion small shapes lying beside a trillion others on the beach. And the tiny grain of sand was Happy.

One day, a large green sea turtle found its way to the tiny isle. It had swum for a thousand miles, and needed respite. As it pulled itself out of the surf and onto the beautiful beach, our tiny grain of black sand found itself wedged inside a slight crease on the underside of the turtle's gleaming, wet shell. After a week of rest, the sea turtle again entered the water, and began its travels southward through the warm waves of the blue ocean.

As the turtle traveled through the seas, that one little happy grain of sand began to worry. Its life had rapidly changed. From the unstressed, sunny, quiet times of contemplating its good fortune while lying on the beach of the beautiful isle, to the uncertainty of life while clinging to the underside of the shell of a green sea turtle. What might happen to it? What if it fell off during a raging storm and drifted for eternity in the endless ocean? What if it got washed to the bottom of the sea, never to be seen again? What if the turtle was eaten by a shark, and the grain of sand would then spend dark days deep in its belly? The list of concerns went on and on. Worry changed into anxiety… and anxiety became panic. Life had become scary and very, very uncertain.

The turtle moved steadily onward with the strong movement of the ocean currents. It seemed to have a destination in mind. Occasionally, it would just drift along upon the currents to save its energy, but mostly, the strong, resilient sea turtle moved with purpose and intention.

It was during the seventeenth week of the voyage at sea that an island came into view. The turtle swam toward it. As it entered the island's protected cove, the color of the water changed from deep turquoise to a brilliant emerald green. Golden streaks of sunlight filtered through the water. The turtle swam with intent toward a dark cave that was protected by ancient island trees. The jungle around it was thick. As it entered the cave, the black grain of sand trembled with fear. It was terrified. What lies ahead? It was all so unsettling. Why was this happening to him?

In this brilliantly written life manual of Inspiration and Hope, *Soul Experience: the 4th Level of Identity*, Al Killeen masterfully provides a compass point, a North Star, for us to discover our truest Identity, and provides clear steps to move beyond day-to-day surviving to thriving during times of fear, worry, and anxiety. That is, in this wonderful book, we are taught how to **thrive** in the **Face of Daily Life**. Killeen invites each of us to ask a very personal question about our deepest level of interaction with the planet, and answer it honestly. At this moment, "Are you Happy?" If that question was asked of the little grain of sand, at its moment of entering the cave on the underside of a green sea turtle, the answer would unquestionably be "no." The black grain of sand had for weeks, since embarking upon its odyssey, experienced a variety of negative emotions, including nervousness, anxiety, and depression. It was unsettled, trembling, and terrified.

In this cutting-edge work, which is the follow-up to his acclaimed book, *Soul Proprietorship: 8 Critical Steps to Overcoming Problems in Business and Life*, Killeen observes that, like many of us, this little grain of sand is operating from Level 3 Identity, the level of Resisting Life. At this level of identity, we align with our ego-Self, whereby we experience the psychological states of fear, worry, and apprehension. The events of the day ***outside of our control*** affects the moods, emotions, and cognitive experiences of one who is engaged in Level 3 Identity. Our ego-state is always vulnerable. Daily life becomes a struggle. We lose our self-esteem, and feel uncertain about our ability to cope. Each moment is lived from a place of expecting the "next dreadful thing to happen to us." *Soul Experience: the 4th Level of Identity*, reveals that it is a subconscious focus on our ego-needs that creates these moments of resistance and hopelessness. Killeen offers keen insights into time-tested ways to move consistently from Level 3 functioning to Level 4 Identity, where you "stay deeply grounded in your inner, larger, eternal Self," a place of Hope, Inspiration, Creativity, Courage, Selfless Service and Love. Killeen offers the poignant wisdom of a Sage, who noted that "When you let go of fear, all that is left is love."

Soul Experience: the 4th Level of Identity clearly explains how to live according to your Highest Self, which is your True Way, when faced with daily events of life, including adversity and desperation. This then leads to a consistent, fearless way to approach all of life's situations. Killeen presents examples and insights, with easy to follow exercises, on how to practice and implement Level 4 Identity that is in accord with one's highest truths. And you get to experience how it feels to succeed when integrating Level 4 Identity.

With a wealth of career expertise, which has been distilled from decades of experience as an Empowerment Mastery Coach, Al Killeen has expertly integrated his own life experiences with insights about such primal questions as "What is your life purpose?" and "Who are you in your deepest way of life and spirit?" He presents deep reflections on such topics as the soul, spirituality, life, death, relationships, religion, marriage, and business. His generous offering of quotes and notations from a host of experts and Masters, in a variety of fields, allows the reader to discover pearls of wisdom from around the globe and across the ages.

Throughout this treatise, Killeen teaches us how to develop our own Personal Life Vision as a way of genuinely interfacing with the planet. This is based on a powerful core theme that authenticity, integrity, and alignment with our Highest Self is the only way to true happiness. The author implores us to dedicate and commit ourselves to living out our sacred path, and finding our highest purpose. A Personal Life Vision provides a guiding beacon that keeps us consistently on the Path, regardless of the circumstances in which we find ourselves. This seminal book outlines the critical steps necessary for pursuing and achieving this goal.

Soul Experience: the 4th Level of Identity is filled with profound ideas and tips for maintaining an internal world of Love and Light, despite daily turbulent experiences which occur "out there." I am reminded of Mother Teresa's words that she would not fight for peace, but rather she would "**Be Peace**." Or Gandhi's message of **being** the light that one wants to see expressed in the world. Killeen shows us the way to achieve this grand purpose. He guides us, through this book, and in his mastery coaching practice, how to arrive there. This is the wisdom of Al Killeen.

Killeen leads us to a deeper level of Conscious Awareness through his use of enlightening stories and descriptions.

These stories help develop greater understanding and insights to promote life change. For example, Killeen presents the story of a wise Holy Man who is confronted by many potentially damaging, stressful events during his sacred life-path. In each situation, the Sage would maintain his composure and peaceful demeanor and answer with the words, "How interesting." This exemplified his higher level of consciousness and awareness, as manifested through a Level 4 Identity. From this place, one's reaction is hope, trust, love, and understanding. Fearlessness is the result. By contrast, fearfulness and hopelessness (i.e., resistance) underlie the desperation found in the Ego-Self's Level 3 Identity. Killeen emphasizes that living fully in Level 4 Identity is the only way to overcome obstacles and solve problems... maintaining alignment with your Authentic, Eternal Self.

And, what became of our little grain of sand and the courageous sea turtle? Upon entering the cave, they were met by a tremendous gathering of joyous sea creatures from around the Seven Seas that were celebrating their arrival. An elderly woman walked over to greet them. She looked as old as the Ages. It was clear, by looking upon her face, that she exemplified love and wisdom. She also radiated peace and deep understanding. In her very Essence, she manifested the loving Spirit of the Island. And, she was smiling... a beautiful, shining smile. "Come and join the celebration," she said, "We have been waiting for you."

The cave had been decorated, lined from floor to ceiling with brilliantly colored grains of sand from throughout the Cosmos. Some of the colors in attendance had not ever been seen before. But something essential had been missing. A black grain of sand. Now, the sea turtle and the beautiful black grain of sand had arrived. Everything was in place for the celebration.

"Why are they celebrating?" the little grain of sand asked. Sliding off the underside of the turtle's shell, it joined a trillion other grains of sand.

The Wise, Sage Woman of the Island answered, "For over ten thousand years we have been gathering together, very deliberately, all of the colors of the Universe in this place. Each represents the greater Truths and Wisdoms that are being revealed to us. We have been waiting for your beautiful black color to arrive. Your color will allow us all to live together in the Awakened Spirit, with Love and Hope. You have brought it to us today! Don't you see? One can't live a purpose-filled life from a place of fear, uncertainty, and worry. One can only live fully and freely when the worries, frets, and anxieties of the Ego-Self drop away, and what remains are one's deepest Truths and Connection with your Higher, Eternal Self. This is the Place of Awareness where one can never be harmed or injured… a place of Empowerment and Fulfillment. Once you experience this, you will never be the same again. It is like discovering the most beautiful pearl in existence. This is the Place where you live with hope, boldness, trust, courage, and resiliency, knowing that you are enough. **A Place where you have permission to be totally immersed in Love and Hope. And in that Place, you are free.**"

The Wise, Sage Woman of the Island continued. "You, my beautiful black grain of sand, harbor the deepest Essence of Love and Hope. And you didn't even know it. Instead, you focused on the worries of your ego-identity, which is always one of fear. You ask, 'Am I good enough? Will I be ok? How do I compare with others?' You have a far greater level of transcendence within than you realize. Don't be afraid. Embrace Abundance and Fearlessness. Be your Highest Self… Love and Hope."

As the grain of black sand touched the ground, suddenly a rainbow of incredibly beautiful, dazzling colors burst forth. Each of the trillion grains of sand shined radiantly. The brilliant light cascaded outward, projecting high onto the ceiling of the cave. It stretched outside into the tropical sky, then beyond the horizon, and far into the Galaxies. In that dazzling moment, a striking metamorphosis occurred. A transcendence. In awe, the black grain of sand realized that its earlier insecurities, fears, worries, and anxieties had been holding it back from living fully… from discovering its Truest Self and Highest Identity. Courage, Fearlessness, Hope, and Love were at the Core of its

Larger, Endless, Inner, Eternal Self. This realization led to a feeling of tremendous Peace and Serenity. Everything was as it should be... nothing left undone. Enlightenment. Love. Hope.

The Wise, Sage Woman of the Island asked, "Are you Happy?"

The beautiful little black grain of sand smiled widely and simply replied, "How interesting."

—Allen D. Brandon, Ph.D.
Founder and President
Rocky Mountain Neuropsychological Sciences, PC
Fort Collins, Colorado

INTRODUCTION

*By becoming "nothing," you experience
that you are "everything."*

You have questions—about your life, your career, your relationships, God, morality, and even what it all means. Are you merely a lucky, advanced animal who was cursed with advanced rational abilities that invite such questions that have no answers?

Are you a Divine Spirit having a human experience and who has just temporarily forgotten who you are?

Does it even matter that you are here?

Of course it does, and of course your life has meaning, but that meaning is elusive and perhaps never to be discovered unless you do the work that reveals it. This book is your invitation to that work.

You may be like me and have read countless books that proclaim to have answers for you. Many of them even had answers that moved your inquiry forward for you a little bit. One or two books may even seem to have contained all the answers in them for you, so you commit to those books and that body of information with your life.

If you read this book carefully, if you practice what is in this book conscientiously, you will find the answers you are seeking to whatever questions you have that have evaded you in life so far. I promise you.

I know this is true because it happened for me. Prove it to yourself by trying what this book guides you to try, and see if your life isn't transformed and if you don't feel solutions to the answers you seek.

Christ said, "These things I do, you can do... and more." Buddha said, "Don't believe me; try it for yourself and prove its truth in your own experience of life." That is the spirit this information is inviting you into by reading and practicing what is within it—beyond mere *belief*, which is comforting when things are going fine, but which usually evaporates in the face of real challenge.

You can be your own salvation, your own guru, your own source of light. Why? Because this book will connect you with what is divine within you, and it has all answers that you seek.

Please note: In this book, terms such as *God, Source, Universe, Tao,* and *Divinity* are used throughout, and you, the reader, should interpret that to mean whatever name you have for that higher source, that overarching force that is the origin of all material and spiritual reality.

WHO YOU NEED TO BE TO OPTIMIZE THIS BOOK AS YOU READ IT

What you experience as you read this book will, in itself, be a reflection of whether you are on Level 3 or Level 4 Identity (which I explain in detail in the following pages) in that particular moment you are reading it. Your life will change each time you read it, and perhaps even as you're reading it. How does that work?

Imagine that one day you are tired and in sort of a cynical mood as you pick up this book. As you read the words and the concepts, your mind will naturally default to your Level 3 Identity. One of the baseline filters of Level 3 Identity is comfort and survival. It's what drives Level 3 ego-based identity with most decisions on the front end. Is this information, situation, or person a friend or foe? Survival. It's critical to all of us. But the ego makes survival its primary job. While we are all used to the idea that we *are* our egos, remember as you read this that you are more than just your ego. And also remember that the ego makes it its primary job for you to survive, but has an even higher priority on its *own* survival, which sometimes isn't what is best for you.

What does reading a book have to do with survival? If the information in the book is different enough from what you previously believed to be true, the ego can interpret that information as threatening at the subconscious level. Now that there is an unrecognized but ever-present threat to what you already previously believed before reading this book, you may deploy cynical judgment to fight with the information to prove that it is not true, thereby relieving discomfort for your ego, which is grounded in your previous paradigm of belief.

However, at Level 4, things change. Imagine that you picked up the book while in a mind-set and heart-set of gratitude. If gratitude is one of your core values, and you personify that commitment to being gratitude, not just being grateful, then reading a book like this will be experienced differently. If you were to read this book as a commitment to gratitude, your open-mindedness to new concepts that may threaten old concepts will be dramatically expanded.

Accordingly, this information may change the paradigm of how you see reality, and will not be labeled and judged as wrong, but rather it will inspire and motivate you to grow further awareness and depth of understanding to expand your knowledge. So, in a sense, you will get the most value out of this book if you are a learner, rather than being a knower.

Same book, same information, but experienced and used or dismissed based upon what level of identity you, the reader, are reading it from.

So I'm going to make an unusual request of you. I'm going to request that you suspend your skeptical mind as you read this book. You may not even realize that you have such a thing, but we all do. If you are willing to suspend your skeptical mind and instead read this book, whenever you read it, through a mind of *possibility*, you will absorb the depth of its inner meaning, and you will be transformed accordingly.

Consider this: maybe you are reading this book not just because it came across your path, but because it was designed to come across your path and help you learn and practice the information within it.

This book may seem like another self-help book. Or spiritual book. Or life coaching book. Or some other genre you could put a label on. But I promise you, this book is the culmination of my fifty years of broad, yet focused, research in the realm of human consciousness and why we are here, and what to do with the fact that we are here.

As you read this book, remember that there are many people who go through experiences similar to your own. It is not in the experience of life that we are automatically doomed to either happiness or suffering, it is through what we do with that experience in our minds—how we process it, judge it, use or dismiss it, fight it or love it, and ultimately whether or not we integrate the deep but subtle messages within our life experience into our own physical, mental, emotional, and spiritual progress.

Our minds are far larger and far more mystical than mere cognitive analytics and the survival-motivated processing of problems. Our minds go far beyond our brains. If you simply are open, conceptually try on the information that follows, and then actually practice what is described in the book that follows, and I promise you a transformed life.

And not just transformation for the sake of transformation, mind you, but transformation into greater knowledge, experience, and fulfillment and power on your path of physical existence, however long or short that path may be. First message of this book for you to try on is this: *it isn't how long you live or how "successful" you are in your life that ultimately matters, it is how deep and significantly you are living that really matters.*

May your path be lit by the wisdom that you awaken.

ARE YOU HAPPY?

Are you happy? Or are you still in pursuit of that one? How about successful? Are you successful? If not, why not? And if you are, is there anything more than that?

Even if you are happy and successful, I can tell you that that isn't enough to satisfy the deepest part within you. There will still be something missing.

This book will tell you not only how to move to happiness, and then beyond it to something more important, but also how to achieve success and then move to something beyond that as well.

If you have a void within you, which 98 percent of people seem to have 90 percent of the time, this book will give you the missing 10 percent that you are seeking and that most people never find.

I hope you choose to read the whole book and find out who you really are and why you are really here.

If you read and practice the principles in this book, I guarantee that your life will change for the better while you are executing your daily, yearly, and lifetime activities. But more importantly, you will find that place of meaning, purpose, inner peace with life, and self-acceptance that evades the vast majority of people who have ever lived.

You will discover the reason you are here in the first place.

POP QUIZ

Take some time in the next hour or two to quietly explore this question: "Am I happy?" If you get any insights, intuitions, or ideas from asking, start a journal and write your responses there. There will be numerous Pop Quizzes as you proceed through this book, which will help your journey if you decide to participate.

MY PERSONAL LIFE VISION

My Personal Life Vision is a world where all people realize their fullest potential,

of extraordinary relationships and extraordinary accomplishments,

where integrity and honorable actions are courageously pursued, and commonly experienced.

What does this mean?

"My Personal Life Vision" means that what I am declaring to the God/Universe, the world and myself that what I am about to write is my most inspired vision for life and my commitment to do, be, and act according to whatever is written next is my largest dream, commitment, and responsibility to create to the best of my ability with the rest of my life.

"Where all people realize their fullest potential" means that I want everyone who lives now and will ever live to become all that they can possibly become spiritually, physically, mentally, emotionally, relationally, occupationally, and healthily. Further, I am to be a force to help that happen to that level with everyone I may ever have any influence on for whatever reason, the rest of my life, to the very best of my ability.

"Of extraordinary relationships and extraordinary accomplishments" means that I am committing to be a force to help anyone and everyone I may be able to influence in any way to have the power, ability, and effectiveness at creating extraordinarily wonderful relationships and accomplish extraordinary things with their time on earth.

"Where integrity and honorable actions are courageously pursued, and commonly experienced" means I am committed to helping everyone in the world practice integrity and honor in all that they say and do with courage and consistently to the best of their ability, and that they also experience the same coming back to them from others.

Why should you care?

Because everything I just wrote is my commitment to you, personally. Because if you read this book, I promise that my Personal Life Vision will actually impact your life in transformational ways.

How?

Because the intentionality behind this book is rooted in my Level 4 Identity, which is embodied in my Personal Life Vision and its intention toward you, the reader.

Why does that matter?

Because everything that manifests out of the human mind begins with intentionality that is then activated through actions and interface and influence. My Personal Life Vision has absolutely, unconditionally, transformed my life for the better by living it as my reminder of how to operate at what I'm about to describe to you.

Most importantly, my Personal Life Vision can be the catalyst to awaken your Personal Life Vision. And as that happens, you discover who you really are—what your "Soul" really is—and that the two are not separate, but the same.

This book will introduce you to your Soul, your true identity.

I

FINDING THE ACTUAL YOU

Universal Mind is perfection without images.
It is far beyond the world of thought.

Divine Mind is undisturbed and exists eternally.

—Buddha

Being a human being is interesting. Very interesting. Beyond any term other than that, we begin to compromise our deepest potential understanding with labels, projections, judgments, opinions, self-validations, and other distractions.

A favorite story I repeat to friends or clients on a seemingly daily basis captures this great truth far better than I can by merely declaring it.

Five hundred years ago in a small village in northern India, a fifteen-year-old girl fell in love with a fifteen-year-old boy, and they did what fifteen-year-olds in love often do. As a result, she discovered that she was pregnant. Horror of horrors! If she told her parents what actually happened, they would exile the disgraced boy from the village, and she would never see him again! So she came up with another plan.

The very night she discovered that she was pregnant, she ran into her parents' little house, threw herself on the floor in tears, and as her alarmed Mother and Father asked her what was wrong, she despondently cried out, "It's horrible! The Holy Man raped me!"

Now, on the edge of the village lived an old Holy Man whom the villagers revered. The young girl thought that if she blamed him, nothing bad would happen because he was so respected, no one would think to confront him. But she didn't know a parent's unbridled love for their child, so her parents responded in a surprising way. They immediately went out to the street of the village in anger, and with lit torches to guide their way, they rallied the villagers and immediately marched down the dusty road to the Holy Man's humble hut and demanded he come forth.

The enlightened Holy Man came out of his house: "How may I help you, my children?" he quietly asked.

"You can help us by admitting you are a fraud!" declared the angry parents.

"How interesting," he clearly and calmly stated with a slight smile.

"Well, it is more than interesting. You raped our daughter, and now she is pregnant, and you must give up this fraudulent pretense of holiness and marry her and support the coming child," the angry father of the girl demanded. "You are a shameful hypocrite and should live under a cloud of shame the rest of your days."

"How interesting," the Holy Man said once more with a smile.

So he made no more comments, made no more fuss, and defended himself not at all. He married the girl, gave up his religious practices, took multiple menial jobs around the town, and supported the girl and her baby without another word.

He ate but a single bowl of rice each day and used everything else he earned to support them without a word of protest. In fact, he never consummated the marriage, treated her as a manifestation of Divine Mother and treated the boy-child with unconditional kindness and love, all with nothing but quiet honor and spiritual love. He never said a word to her about her lies, nor did the boy he was now raising ever feel anything other than unconditional love from him as an ideal father would have given him.

Finally, after ten years, the girl could take the guilt no more. One night, she threw herself once more on her parents' floor in deep despair and cried out, "I have committed an unpardonable sin. I have accused the innocent Holy Man of raping me and impregnating me, yet it wasn't him. It was my boyfriend who I willingly had sex with who gave me my child."

"What have you done, you crazy girl! You have cast us into hell for sure!" the parents responded in alarm and incredulity. Now deeply ashamed and saddened by their ruination of the poor Holy Man's life, they once more went out into the streets and gathered the townspeople to slowly make their way to the Holy Man's little hut. Throwing themselves into the dirt before it, they began whipping themselves and crying in despair.

The Holy Man came out of his hut and quietly asked, "Children, children, what is wrong?"

"We have ruined your life unfairly," the distraught parents told him. "We know you were innocent, yet you gave up ten years of your spiritual practices and took care of our daughter and grandchild, yet never said a word. What could you possibly have to say to such lowly sinners as us?" the shattered parents asked through their tears.

"How interesting" was all he said, with a quiet smile and a light in his eyes—a light of compassion and forgiveness.

Now, what is the point of that story?

As you read the rest of this book, you will understand. Perhaps you, too, will one day get to a place where, no matter what happens, the superficial "you" in life will stay deeply grounded in your inner Self, your larger Self, your eternal Self, your Level 4 Self—the actual *you*.

When that day comes, like the Holy Man, you will be able to see the ups and downs, victories and defeats, pleasures and pains, oscillations of all experiences of life's dreams as merely "interesting." When you get there (if you aren't already), you will no longer have anything to fear in life.

That day, you will finally have power. You will finally have understanding. You will no longer be controlled by emotions, judgments, and isolation.

You will finally understand love because as another famous Holy Man once stated, "When you let go of fear, all that is left is love."

WHERE TRUE POWER LIES

The meaning of Karma is in the intention.

The intention behind the action is what matters.

Those who are motivated only by the desire

for the fruits of action are miserable,

*for they are constantly anxious about the results
of what they do.*

—Krishna

You are reading this; you are a human being.

As a human being, you are capable of four levels of identity— at least as far as your physically manifested Self is concerned.

Every human being who lives past puberty automatically experiences the first three levels of identity (assuming normal mental development). The bad news is that 98 percent of people never move past the third level of identity to realize the real opportunity of being a human—Level 4 Identity.

However, every human being also has the capacity to come to understand and live from a Level 4 Identity.

Level 4 is where true power lies, and true purpose lies, and where one is fully alive as opposed to "just not being dead."

Level 1: Helplessness
Level 2: Learning
Level 3: Defying and exploring
Level 4: Wisdom, power, and understanding

It takes several skills to be able to live at Level 4:

- Awareness that Level 4 exists

- Courage to pursue Level 4

- Pathology of how to pursue Level 4

- Execution of that pathology of pursuing Level 4

- Adjustments to their execution along the way to improve results

- Resolve to pursue Level 4 until you not only experience it, you *are* it

For those courageous souls who decide that their lives are about living significantly, and not merely successfully, Level 4 is the only real pursuit worth pursuing because it determines their growth of consciousness through all their subsequent external experiences, as surely as ducklings follow their mother to the water.

All else is secondary because living from Level 4 is what makes all else really mean something beyond the mere experience of struggling existence. Living from Level 4 creates a legacy of meaning for your life, and having that meaning determines the contributions you have made and will make to this world. While you may think that doesn't matter right now with all the immediate distractions before you in daily living, I promise you it will become the most important question you will have to answer to when you have five minutes left before this life is over. Therefore, the stewardship with which you practice your life is, arguably, the most important legacy you can stay focused on as the foundation for whatever else you think, intend, or do in this life. You want your life to matter.

You want that. As do I. So let's go become that—and experience wonderment.

2

MY LIFE STORY

That which fuels the fire consumes itself.
—*Lao Tzu*

While we all may feel uniquely flawed or gifted or abnormal or perverse or most likely an ever-shifting combination of those attributes, the fact is that all humans simultaneously experience both uniqueness and oneness from and with other humans. Our life story reveals this interesting interplay of these two seemingly competing themes of our existence. We each have experiences that impact us, and how we respond to them determines how consciously we conclude them to be either curses or blessings or both or beyond either.

Before I begin the story of my life (at least as I tell it to myself), a few truths must be acknowledged:

- This overview is based on selective memory and revisionist personal history, undoubtedly modified by the scripting and emphasis points along the journey.

- Despite my insistent belief that this story somehow is uniquely profound and has messages within it that can guide all people, it is in fact no more unique or profound than anybody else's story—and especially yours.

- While I believe that it matters that you know my story to fully appreciate the messages and information I've generated as a result of its pathway, it's only actual value will be realized to the extent that you care to take the time to look for correlating "truths" for your life and those of others. And I can't force that to happen. Only you can choose to practice the following and let it happen.

Our collective experiences packaged with the timelines of our lives become the stories of our lives. Here's mine:

I was born the youngest of three children to a 1950s American middle-class family. Denver, Colorado, was the place. Lived in a 750-square-foot house with the five of us, directly across from a US Air Force base (one of their trucks ran over my cocker spaniel).

My early years were spent traveling to various states with my family to live based on my dad's government job. I was constantly changing elementary classes, having to figure out and adapt to whatever the micro-culture happened to be in those classes of kids in Phoenix, Reno, Billings, or wherever. Otherwise, I would be the elementary school outcast, which I was anyway due to being the new/strange kid in the room each year.

The early years as a grade school kid taught me several lessons:

- Life isn't always fun, fair, or comprehensible.

- My older sister can go off the rails and run away when I was ten, and I may only see or talk to her a half dozen times in the following fifty years due to how relationships go when they aren't fertilized by common interest or proximity.

- My parents, despite being fine people with noble hearts and intentions toward others, are still capable of giving in to alcoholism, poor financial discipline, addictive self-indulgence in gambling habits, and generally being clueless as to how to optimize their children's futures.

- My older brother can be a compelling personality who seemed as if he could conquer the world with brains and Irish articulation, yet would die in the streets of Boulder, Colorado, in his mid-fifties having succumbed to those alcohol and addictive habits learned and practiced throughout his abbreviated lifetime.

- In the end, I had to find the answers to life's existential dilemmas or I would follow suit with my family's self-destructive tendencies, and those answers weren't going to be found from the same mind-sets that practiced ego-based self-indulgences like my family had unwittingly practiced on their journeys through life.

COLLEGE YEARS: THE BREAKOUT

College was a breakout experience for me in all ways that matter to launch young adulthood. My first year was spent hiding out at a small college high in the mountains of Colorado—the kind of place where kids from the East Coast come to ski and party, and where local Colorado kids go who are generally too insecure to handle a large university experience that may challenge them.

I was one of those.

Then, after my first LSD trip (and only one, thank God), I decided I had nothing to lose by going to a real university, Colorado University. Wow, what a change!

Drugs. Hippies in the streets selling and doing them. Braless girls. Free spirits. Top-level professors. And a huge vine-covered campus to get lost in.

Heaven, hell, challenge, love, broken hearts, sex unbridled, alcohol, drugs, and most significant of all, the roots of purpose and pathway to decide to embrace life rather than just take myself out of it via suicide (which I seriously considered after receiving a B in my favorite class, and thus almost destroying my vision of graduating in four years with straight A's). Working full-time and getting into graduate school to lead to a career as an intellectual history professor.

After graduating in four years, after all, with an A- cumulative grade point average and honors (cum laude in history), I went to grad school to ultimately become a European intellectual history professor. After that first year in grad school, I decided to pull the plug on academia and get out into the world and find out what life was like either in a Zen monastery or in business. I knew that if I stayed, I would be simply hiding out behind university life the rest of my life.

My first real job was for a pharmaceutical company as a sales rep for northern Colorado. It was a drag. Egocentric doctors, a poor product line. Horrific. Simultaneously during this phase, I was practicing serious spiritual work by training to become a Zen monk. Twelve-hour meditations on Sundays, daily practices and readings, attending satsangs regularly, all the trappings of preparation for the monastery. Perhaps, ultimately, just a more exotic form of running away from life as being a professor would have been.

Then I went to work for my eventual wife's business, a health food store. That ended with a dramatic difference of approach to business with my future father-in-law leading me into the mortgage lending industry.

On the personal side of life, I fell in love and asked my wife, Reese, to become so in 1977, but with conditions (what girl doesn't want to hear that?). The conditions were that I wanted the right to leave the marriage at any time to become the Zen monk I had intended to spend my life as, and there were to be no children in the marriage. I decided that I had come from a deeply dysfunctional family and would likely repeat the pattern, thus it would be "safer" to avoid the experience of trying to be a parent and failing at it.

Two kids later (Cameron born in 1988 and Holden born in 1993), I asked my wife why she ever agreed to marry me with those conditions. She told me, "Because I knew you would never become a Zen monk, and I knew I would be the one who would determine if we ever had children." I guess that tells us all who really has the power over destiny in this world when it comes to having or not having children.

As it turns out, I am so grateful she had the wisdom to co-create the boys with me. They, along with she, have become my greatest teachers, although not always in formal or comfortable ways. And I didn't always recognize them as such. In fact, my Level 3 Self often felt anger, resentment, and discouragement toward them along with love, joy, and deep eternal connection. It took my Level 4 Self to see them with more enlightened eyes to understand these truths:

- They were never "mine" in the first place. They were simply part of my path of stewardship that I had co-created with Reese and the larger source behind us all.

- They have a right to learn about life without being my version of "safe" or "smart" or "responsible." In fact, that is the only way they will learn to be self-dependent, as you and I both had to.

- They taught me, along with their mom, what unconditional love could look and feel like, which challenged my courage to try to practice it after their example.

As far as Reese goes, she has been the greatest blessing of my life. She endured my Level 3 self-destructive tendencies and nurtured my Level 4 awakening to meaning and power. If you get one of those in life, never let go of them. Those partners are rare and invaluable.

I worked in mortgage lending from 1977 to 2000, with a brief phase as a stockbroker (which I was really bad at, since I realized that knowledge and intentionality alone weren't enough to create predictable results for clients). Accordingly, I learned a valuable business lesson about the investment markets that no matter how much you believe in various products and talk friends, family, and clients into believing in them too, you will ultimately lose them some money.

Back in mortgage lending in 1984, I humbly vowed to take no more chances with my career or my life. Time to stay underground, I thought to myself. The pain of life outweighed its promise, so I decided to stop inviting that pain as much as possible. I decided. And by deciding, I spent the next six years of my life working hard, being married, and raising children.

Anyway, those six years were, in many ways, years in which I wasn't fully alive. I was just not dead. I was warm, safe, dry—and just existing.

Then, in 1988, a friend proposed we start a mortgage company together. Although scared, I spent a few hours every night reading books to create the courage and wrote a business plan, and in 1990 launched the company with that friend.

We built it from two partners and two administrative employees to fifty, and from $20 million a year in production to

$250 million by the time we sold in 1999, with a 6,000 percent increase of equity from start-up capital.

Along the way in the nineties, I got involved with mortgage industry politics and ended up going through the executive chairs of the Colorado Mortgage Lenders Association to the CEO/President from 1997 to 1998. I experienced the best and worst parts of the political bureaucracy that dominates in all such environments, to some degree or another. During this phase, I was simultaneously CEO of my own company, CEO of the CMLA, and founder/CEO of RMMLA (an eight-state mortgage industry association) designed to give more legislative voice to the fly-over states in the mountain region of America.

As our company grew, all of us partners who owned it didn't. We fought, we disagreed, each nurturing our own private martyrdom in the name of Level 3 self-validation.

At the end of the decade of the nineties, my partners and I decided to sell our company. I found a company that wanted to buy us and we sold it. It was part of a five-company rollup into this larger group. After the sale, the terms of the sale required that I was on a three-year executive contract and doing senior executive work on behalf of all of the companies. That went on for about a year of the three-year contract. Then the world turned on its proverbial axis.

The Tennessee bankers who had bought all five mortgage companies decided they didn't like the kind of money that executives made in the mortgage industry, so they fired us all. At forty-eight years old, I got fired for the first time in my life from the company I founded after having sold it.

After I was fired, I sat in the parking lot of our building that night at sunset while basking in the self-pity of shame, reeling in shock and fear. I was running all of the dark tapes that you might imagine: "I'm a loser, and I've always known I was a loser, but now the world will know that I'm a loser!" As I sat there and I thought over what had happened, I didn't know what to do next. I was paralyzed.

I drove home slowly and sadly to let my wife know that she had bet on the wrong horse and married a loser who could no longer support the family. But my wife, being the noble and quiet saint that she is, did something that night to change my life. She asked me, "Do you still believe what's hanging downstairs in our laundry room?" What she was referring to was a stained glass saying that we had had for decades that said this:

"Your life is a gift from God,

and what you do with it is your gift back to God."

I slowly nodded and told her that I still agreed with that.

"What if there are three to five times in our life when the membrane is thinnest and life is toughest, but those are the moments that, if we push through, we can discover what that gift is that the saying is talking about?" she quietly asked me.

She went on. "And what if this is one of those times? What if this is the moment when you are being challenged to decide what you want to do with your life? What I would like you to do is follow your heart and your passion to whatever it leads you to, and if we lose everything and end up in a trailer somewhere, I will still be with you!"

She both inspired me and shamed me and gave me hope at that moment. She shifted my thinking to what could be, rather than what I feared most. As a result, I decided that there was more here than just giving me an opinion. The Universe was talking to me, and therefore God was—through my wife. So I decided to take a chance on the possibility of my life and created a company that was built around the pragmatic bridging and synthesis of universal spiritual principles translated as values into pragmatic daily application for the purpose of fulfilling the optimal destinies of individuals' lives and organizations.

In doing so, I would be creating a company that would be more than a way to make a living; it would fulfill an inspired synthesis of spiritual, commonsense, business principles, life principles, psychology, and human optimization tools to create fulfilled lives for the people who practiced what it taught. It wouldn't just be a company or a vehicle of commerce. It would be a sacred vessel, a temple for all mankind to become their optimal versions of themselves through being both successful (whatever that means), as well as significant.

I wanted to replace my fear-based relationship with living with a positive and inspired one, not just a responsible one. And I wanted to be able to help anyone who ever interfaced with it to be able to do the same. I wanted to support people and companies by bridging the foundational guidance of values with the pragmatic execution of life and businesses demands while creating individual fulfillment along the journey.

So I started my own company, Integrative Mastery Programs (IMP). It has been, to say the least, the most amazing experience of my life.

Imagine your dream job, a job that awakens and demands the very best of the unique gifts that this life gave you, and by sharing those gifts with clients, you finally find love of life, faith in life, gratitude for life—without conditions—wherever it leads next.

That is what Integrative Mastery Programs has given me. It has shown me who I am, not just what I thought I should be because life, other people, or past experiences and scripts told me I should be in my head.

In an industry where 94 percent of business coaches ultimate fail or barely scratch out a meager living, I fortunately became one of the top 3 percent of business coaches in the world after my first year, and I have been there for going on twenty years now. And the irony is, I may well be one of the most personally screwed up people around, but the process I was allowed to synthesize is truly, uniquely, and inspirationally transformational for all people and companies. (I'm not just saying that, I'll show you.)

I am now humbled and honored to coach around fifty extremely successful people as a life coach. I also get to write books; give speeches, workshops, and programs for individuals and organizations; create and guide spiritual retreats; and support people I meet with an open heart rather than a guarded one.

I am allowed these gifts from life because I approach them as opportunities of stewardship my Level 4 Self invites, and that somehow seems to invite their manifestation in my life and work.

Level 4 does that. It transforms people who practice it into a new relationship with life, business, spiritual endeavors, marriages, parenting, health, relationships, and even death. It does so regardless of the person's background, ethnicity, sexual orientation, gender, or parental/experiential/societal scripting—as long as they practice it in their lives.

Living in Level 4 can transform your life too. So when that life is over in this dimension, you will not have spent your time "just not dead," but rather fully alive. Because you will know why you were here in the first place, before your life is over in this dimension, at long last.

3

NOW IT'S TIME FOR
YOUR STORY

*The sky has no east or west, nor does not make
distinctions between this and that.*

Distinctions arise from the human mind alone.

—Buddha

Now that you've learned a bit about my journey thus
far in life, what about you? And why should an author
be asking you, the reader, about your life anyway?
Have you recently (or ever, for that matter) reviewed the
details of your life and examined how you got this far?

POP QUIZ

Before proceeding, it may be helpful to ask yourself
some questions and answer them in writing, in
private, for your eyes only. Some of those questions
may include the following:

- **What is my detailed life story (not just the normal
highlight reel I always reference, but the actual**

play-by-play of the chapters of my life and how they impacted my thoughts, identity, and behaviors)?

- How have the events of my life along with the people in my life influenced who I think I am and how I operate day-to-day?

- What am I most effective and ineffective at in how I participate in my work, my significant other, my family, my relationships, my spirit walk, my health—my life?

- Who have been the primary influencers in my life, and which of those influencers have been empowering versus disempowering?

- Do I trust myself enough to know that I can endure whatever life sends my way, fully admitting that some of those experiences are going to test my limits of suffering?

- What are my top three self-limiting beliefs?

- Am I committed enough to my life happiness and fulfillment to make any changes necessary to get there?

Please write your answers in your journal you started with your first Pop Quiz answer earlier in the book.

Here's why I am asking you about your story.

This is no mere book. This is a pathway to discovering who you really are, rather than who you thought you were so far this lifetime. And for that to happen, you must first explore the foundation as to who it is that you thought you were before reading this because once you have read this book, you will never look at your life, identity, or purpose in life the same again.

You will be transformed.

You will be eligible to have the power to actually enjoy your life as one of significance, meaning, and passion.

Don't believe me? That would be understandable because if someone claimed what I just did, I wouldn't believe them either.

I have been disappointed too many times. The exaggerated claims, the hype, the bullshit that gets sold every day in the name of transformation. The problem with that hype is this: You can't transform your life from the same identity that is limiting it.

I know. I know. That quote is a rip-off of Einstein's famous quote that "you can't solve a problem from the same level of consciousness that created it" adapted to this context, but it is true nonetheless.

This book will show you how to become an identity that is the highest version of *you*, and that is critical if you are to ever feel differently about life than you do today. You will experience love and gratitude and success/significance at levels you never could have imagined.

I know, not only because of the work I have done for the past forty-five years, but more importantly because I have lived it. Now, let's explore the Four Levels of Identity together.

4

THE FOUR LEVELS OF IDENTITY: AN OVERVIEW

As we become Sages,

our minds begin to see the Oneness of all things,

our bodies become more flexible and supple,

and our hearts soften in love.

You can train your mind through meditation, reading and mental exercise. You can train your body through Yoga, Tai Chi and physical exercise. You can train your heart through listening, accepting... and forgiving all.

—*Lao Tzu*

I could share with you that the four levels of identity as a paradigm of human development have been shared with numerous mental health experts, and they agree it is true. Or I could just as easily tell you to simply imagine the following information is true. Both of which are just perspectives to help open you up to that information.

It doesn't ultimately matter either way. What matters is that you read the concepts carefully and then practice using that information in your life domains.

The Buddha had an interesting statement when he said, "Don't believe me just because I say it, but rather test it all in your own life experience to prove it to yourself." Additionally, he warned us with his final words before death: "All is in change constantly; therefore, work on your own salvation with diligence."

What was this man's message that he had spent forty years teaching in India 2,500 years ago after achieving enlightenment? To me, at least, it warns us that this life is a temporary chapter in a much larger version of who we really are. And that chapter must be taken seriously and guided with great mental stewardship.

So I am imploring you to read this book in a different way than you read most books like this. I am requesting that you take a chance that this is not just another self-help book, but rather information that you are to receive at this time to offer you what is perhaps one last chance to make of your life what it has the capacity to become.

If you do that, your entire view of life will change, and that shift alone will transform your destiny from where it is currently going into where it could go.

Be bold. Read and practice—with diligence.

So what are the four levels of identity? And how do you get to that sacred, empowered, and rarely lived place of Level 4?

LEVEL 1 IDENTITY: BEGINNING

AGE PHASE: Birth to approximately three months

DESCRIPTOR: Undifferentiated Disempowered Self

DEFINITIONS: Undifferentiated (part of an indefinable whole; not separate from anything else), disempowered (lacking in power to do anything through free will), Self (who you believe yourself to be, as well as who you actually are whether you recognize it or not)

DETAILS: A newborn baby is born into this new paradigm of reality. It is shocking! Loud noise, bright lights, bodily sensations of warmth and cold, other people, noises they make to communicate (language), and this Level 1 baby lacks the cognitive development to make much sense of it all.

It would be like suddenly finding yourself on a foreign planet with aliens all around you with powers and communication abilities that make no sense to you, and you are a helpless new being on this planet who can't walk, talk, or relate to those aliens.

What are the focal points in this first level of identity? To seek pleasure and avoid pain, at least to the best of your ability. Actually, at this stage of development, a Level 1 child largely just reacts to both states.

When pleasure is experienced, a Level 1 baby may smile, laugh, giggle, coo, or simply sleep. On the other hand, when pain is experienced the baby will cry, fuss, or kick and thrash their limbs in response.

Either way, this level is one of great helplessness and minimal power in response to either pleasure or pain by any associated actions that induce one or the other. Accordingly, this level is the least empowered.

Why is this level called undifferentiated as a Self at this level? Because there doesn't exist an awareness of separateness from others on a conscious and useful level. All is simply one experience amid the ocean of flowing experiences of the pleasure/pain oscillation. For example, does a fish know it is a fish? No, it doesn't. Why? Because only humans require language that labels things, and also has self-consciousness.

Fish don't know they are anything separate from anything else, because the very notion of "separate" is a conceptual process that higher-functioning humans automatically indulge in, and fish do not. Accordingly, fish are undifferentiated too, because they have no paradigm of separation from other fish or from their experiences, just like newborn babies.

Why is this level considered disempowered? Because no self-guided power to produce results through one's own intentions, actions, or efforts occurs at this level; all is seemingly magical and beyond the baby's choice and control.

This is the foundational level for a whole and empowered life that, ironically, begins so humbly and lacks any self-empowered intentions or activities. As discouraging as it is, it is critical because such a state invites the caretaking from a parent or older, conscious person to aid this helpless infant in the face of their helplessness, and that defines how the future adult will *be*, growing out of this infant experience of love, connection, helplessness, and trust. (Most serial killers share a lack of love and bonding at this stage and, as a result, lack a conscience later in life that would otherwise be a barrier to acting out violent impulses against others.)

There is no better way to relate to infants in Level 1 Identity than to practice patient, loving, and consistent attention and care as they develop. To do this is to begin scripting the consciousness of that infant into a healthy relationship with love, confidence, morality, and connection to other people over a lifetime.

LEVEL 2 IDENTITY: LEARNING

AGE PHASE: Three months to puberty

DESCRIPTOR: Compliant Ego-Based Self

DETAILS: An infant grows aware of his or her hands and feet at some point, often around three to four months of age. They begin to, at first, roll over accidentally using these appendages. Then they realize they can control that activity and begin to do so by intention. Simultaneous with this general phase of growth, Mom and Dad are constantly making this sound toward the infant while looking into their eyes and usually comforting, cooing at them, or smiling or kissing them and saying the child's name.

What's in a name? Well, one thing it does is create an automatic connotation with self-identity, so when a mom keeps smiling at her baby and says the sound "John," it eventually occurs to the baby that she is talking to "me" when she makes that sound (Pavlovian conditioned response; linking two sensations together). So, suddenly, the baby thinks that whenever I hear the sound "John," I look at where it is coming from and begin to think that person is talking to "me."

Now there is a "me."

That is the crossover point, the point at which Level 2 Identity is rooted in the existential realization in this heretofore new and mystical reality I find myself in. There is now "me" and "not me." There is now "John" and "not John." And my body is the extent of "John," with everything outside of that body being "not John."

All of those things, places, people, and environmental elements around me that are "not John" can give me either pleasure or pain. I want more of one and less of the other, so I develop into a willing learner from (in this example) being "John" living in a "not John" reality that has the power to give me either pleasant or unpleasant subsequent experiences.

So, I better figure out the rules of this new place. And I want pleasure (and approval from others, particularly my parents, siblings, and others in my "family"), so I willingly become "compliant."

So now, little John, or anyone at this stage of life, willingly begins to drink in information to find out how to get more pleasure, more approval, more comfort, more fun (and less of their opposites).

How do they do that?

They go through a phenomenal phase of gathering information by listening to, being conditioned by, being taught by, and being influenced by countless institutions and experiences of influence around them: parents, siblings, relatives, teachers, ministers, cartoons, movies, books, hot stoves, ice cream, pain, ecstasy, life experiences of all kinds.

They become compliant, ego-based selves. The ego is born and with it, the next phase of our evolution in this life.

POP QUIZ

Take some time in the next three hours and close your eyes and remember the top three memories you have from this phase of your life, this experience of your Level 2 Identity, and how they impacted you at the time. Write down your insights in your journal.

LEVEL 3 IDENTITY: RESISTING

AGE PHASE: Puberty to death or to Level 4

DESCRIPTOR: Noncompliant Ego-Based Self

DETAILS: As the sex hormones begin to awaken in large amounts within the prepubescent child's body, he or she begins to have new chemistry internally, and, with it, certain tendencies grow strong. Those tendencies include

- The desire to have sexual experiences,

- The retreating willingness to continue to merely comply with the directives of outside institutional authorities for compliance and acceptance,

- The beginning of experimentation with his or her own moral and societal code based on new influences, scripting from peers, and acceptance by sexually attracted opposites,

- The dramatic growth of the "trunk of evidence" hidden in our lives where we house all our mistakes, shameful acts, guilts, and dark secrets that we hope never get discovered by others (because if they were ever found, we couldn't possibly be "love-worthy"), and

- A tremendous surge in outside-to-in reactivity to people, their opinions, situations, environments, and influencers outside of our original circle of trust we held at a younger stage of identity. We become more volatile, insecure with whom we have been, emotional, uncertain, and reactive to situations.

Level 3 is best captured by the insecurity of middle school. Remember standing in front of the mirror for hours on end trying to desperately hide the imaginary (or real) pimple or blemish that we just knew everybody would see.

This is a stage of drama. It is a critical phase of life that allows us to develop our own pathology of understanding and development of unique identity, and it is entirely appropriate in the teen years, the twenties, and perhaps even the thirties. By the forties, however, it begins to grow old.

Consider the constant sensitivity to how we imagine others are judging us (which is actually just a reflection of our own harsh self-judgments projected onto others in many cases). The constant projection of ominous outcomes in the future based on problems we are experiencing today. The insecurity of the future without the routine of stability, security, and trust of parents or other institutions making it "safe."

These are all manifestations of this vital phase of growth, but it is not without its dark side.

It is in this phase when most of us begin our experimentation with activities, thoughts, and pursuits that may well create future dark consequences. Drugs, alcohol, irresponsible sexual activity, risky temptations of physical endangerment—all are often introduced into our experience in this phase of our lives. It is also in this phase where we create the foundation of whom we will be the rest of our lives once we are outside of the controlling influences of those people who have controlled our reality up to this point (our family, in most cases).

The "pear must drop from the tree" in this phase (establishing independence beyond the nuclear family and creating our own lives), and the decisions as to what that "pear" will look like on its own is ripe with mistakes, challenges, uncertainty, and insecurity.

And all of those mistakes and false experimentations add another "rock" into the trunk of evidence against ourselves hidden away from the world—but not hidden from ourselves.

These "rocks" or evidence of our personal perceived sins, guilts, and mistakes weigh us down over time, tremendously. And the weight of these slowly grow our tendency to avoid risks, slow or even stop our growth, and limit our futures by our past mistakes. We settle for the limited self-acceptance available to us after our subconscious persecution from this "trunk of evidence."

The second great evolution out of this level of identity is the tendency to begin living outside-to-in. What, exactly, is outside-to-in living? Reactive living, rather than proactive living (which is inside-to-out living).

Outside-to-in or reactive living is the tendency to constantly monitor our environment, both real and imagined, and consider whether it represents a benefit, a threat, or neither to our current reality. What are some examples?

- The weather is gray and cloudy outside as a winter storm approaches, and the landscape seems dead and dreary (environment); I react to it with dark thoughts about how horrible winter is and how dead and hopeless it all seems (reaction).

- My best friend tells me I am a horrible person because I didn't call her back last night after our dinner together (social rejection); I react to it with anger at her, or depression and guilt about myself (reaction).

- My business has a major setback and is losing buckets of money in a way that threatens its continued viability (environment); I turn hostile to my employees for not watching the bottom line enough and force them to quit out of my abusive behavior, accelerating the downward slide of the business (reaction).

- My wife tells me I am lazy and drink too much (social rejection); I ruminate on what a bitch she is and how she is lucky I ever married her (reaction).

- My favorite political party loses an election and I now know that the country is going down the tubes (environment). I grow depressed (reaction).

These are just a few examples of the countless times we let outside-to-in thinking create a life of constant pressure, stress, anger, uncertainty, and a host of other emotions.

We don't necessarily *know* we are reacting that way, and in fact we usually make a strong case for simply being victims within it, but the result is the same: disempowerment, disconnection, disillusion, and a lack of joy about life.

This is not an abnormal way for people to relate to life. In fact, as measured by how commonplace it is, it is the most normal way for people to interface with life (at least as measured by the percentage of how often most adults practice it, which I estimate at 98 percent, whether we are aware of it while it is happening or not at our subconscious level).

And, here's the disturbing news: such reaction only gets more predominant with time and age if nothing redirects it, like evolving to Level 4 (which will be covered in subsequent chapters).

What happens if we don't move from Level 3 to Level 4 as we age? You might think of it as a bell curve of experience that starts out with ascension through experience and power and options as we grow from our teens to our twenties, and to our thirties, and into our forties. Generally, this is the phase of life where people are getting married, having children, and building careers.

During this building phase of our young adulthood, we have little reason to believe that our Level 3 Identity is not who we are. However, as we approach middle age, the rocks of evidence that we have gathered along our path of experience begin to weigh us down so much that we begin to subtly, and often subconsciously, undermine our relationship with self-acceptance and self-trust.

The net effect of this decline may be one reason that people experience middle-age crazy. What is that? What is this phenomenon that affects so many people getting approximately halfway through their lives only to find that they are disappointed with the trajectory of those lives?

I personally believe that middle-age crazy is our larger identity, our Soul Identity. Our Level 4 Identity is trying to come out and save us from a predictably disappointing future if we do not awaken and practice it. That predictable future, while perhaps being warm, safe, and dry, will prove to be increasingly unfulfilling, empty, and discouraging and will ultimately invite simple endurance of the experience of life rather than fulfillment within it. While this certainly isn't everyone's experience during this phase all the time, you may be saying to yourself, "My life is pretty happy. What is this guy talking about?"

However, consider what drove Siddhartha to leave his life of luxury and comfort to find the answers to existence leading to his awakening (his Buddha-hood). Old age, sickness, and death, which awaits us all. And with those guaranteed experiences of misery before us if we live long enough, the suffering built into an unconscious life will become more and more apparent with time, even if we aren't experiencing it at this moment.

As we exit our teens, twenties, and thirties and move into middle age and beyond, the dark side of Level 3 Identity becomes more and more apparent. We are no longer as excited about the things that excited us earlier in life, and by now we have enough scars of disappointment to make us a little more careful and a little more leery. Responsibilities can begin to seem like imprisoning parameters that determine what we are going to be the rest of our days.

As we go on in life and we hopefully establish greater financial security on our path, we often seek stimulating experiences to break the tedium of daily, ever-expanding responsibilities and routine. Those stimulating experiences might be travel, addiction to drugs or alcohol, different hobbies, or simply doubling down on becoming workaholics until we are no longer able to work.

It is in the trunk of evidence over in the corner where we begin gathering even more quiet despondencies and guilts and shames against ourselves with such fervency as we grow older through our Level 3 Identity. As a result, the trunk gets ever heavier. We are increasingly saddened by how many bad things we believe we have done. Our shames, our guilts and sins all ride with us like so many heavy monkeys on our back. And the trunk is now getting big enough that it's getting harder and harder to hide it from other people so that we can avoid their judgment.

I'm not saying there aren't happy times and some joy and some ecstasy while at Level 3 Identity. To be sure, there are happy experiences along the way for most people. But the pendulum-like momentum of pleasant to unpleasant, doubt to faith, suffering to peace pattern gets old. Quietly, in the dead of night and within that echo chamber of our midnight minds, we secretly wonder: "How can I ever enjoy the good times knowing that the bad times are sure to follow, and soon?"

Further, as we get older, we know that the balance of joy is likely to shift, if for no other reason than our physical health and energy are declining. Level 3 can be hell for a lot of people, and nearly purgatory for others, but rarely, if ever, heaven for any of us.

POP QUIZ

Close your eyes and remember the top two or three experiences from your teen years that impacted you, and if you are old enough the same two or three top experiences when you were in your twenties, thirties, forties, and subsequent decades. Write these moments down for each of those phases of your life, including what happened and how you responded at the time and how it ultimately turned out. Put your insights in your journal please.

LEVEL 4 IDENTITY: AWAKENING

AGE PHASE: Awakening (whenever that happens in life), until death (and perhaps beyond)

DESCRIPTOR: Undifferentiated, Empowered, Values-Based Self

DETAILS:

- Upon awakening the awareness of the existence of Level 4 Identity, there is now an option beyond the predictable cycle of ego and its limitations for one's identity and destiny. If tried and practiced, it becomes ever more clear that this is *the* level of fulfillment and power we all seek, but very few find. This is our Soul Identity that we can experience while in human form.

- That identity is now "undifferentiated" because people operating from Level 4 have a larger sense of Self. That Self is no longer merely rooted in the physical and personality and experiential identity of the individual. It now identifies with entities outside of its physical existence as being a part of itself. That includes other people, animals, nature, the earth, the universe, and the Source itself.

- That identity is empowered because it now operates with larger resources of empowerment than its own inclinations and tendencies intrinsic to an ego-based identity. It is empowered, in fact, because its filter for intentions, decisions, and actions is now values as opposed to personal comfort and ego gratification, which means it becomes intrinsically more universal in its view than the self-serving filter that the ego requires as part of its own survival.

- At this level of identity, several critical elements of existence shift that also contribute to the new level of empowerment. One of the first of these element shifts that occurs is that the tendency of outside-to-in reactivity that is innate at Level 3 ego-based identity is reversed, and a Level 4 Identity person begins to live inside-to-out instead. What does this mean? It means that people at Level 4 are now entrusted with power to become, in Hindu terminology, "a creator of worlds," as opposed to a mere reactor to life circumstances due to an unchallenged fealty to being comfortable as the primary priority.

As we practice this power of being able to manifest what we want in life rather than merely react to outside circumstances, and we do so through the filter of values, we tend to be supportive, loving, and impactful in the lives of those around us. As strange as it may seem, my conclusion is that *Divinity/God/Source can now trust us with the power to manifest because we are doing it for reasons beyond those that are self-serving.* Accordingly, we can be trusted with profound power to manifest a future unlimited by the past that makes a huge difference in relieving the suffering of others and, in doing so, provides fulfillment and less suffering at a deep level within us.

- Values-based Self means that the self-image and self-identity for an individual is not based on their name, image in the world, personality, or experiences. This is a Self that personifies and embodies values in any moment in time in the way that that person thinks, intends, and acts. I believe that the secret to being entrusted with power is due to the individual operating out of this larger sense of Self. After all, when a person is operating out of the identity and intentions of personified values, they are operating in a way that connects with other people who share those values. This so-called connection has those other people feeling a sense of oneness with that person, beyond the standard barriers of egoistic differentiation. Accordingly, a person operating as an expression of values and out of this level of Self creates entirely different responses from life and other people along the journey of their path forward.

I can honestly say from my experience in life that awakening Level 4 is personal salvation (at least in a worldly and secular sense).

In fact, it may even be part of what being "born again" was referenced to by Christ when he invited people to align themselves with Him. That is, of course, a reference to the Christian belief in salvation. But even if you are not a Christian, it does not preclude you from the seemingly universal sense of emptiness that grows in life for most people that makes a new beginning desirable in hopes of filling that growing void.

If a person doesn't find a new way, a new path, and a new view of life through the divine eyes within them (as opposed to the mere ego-based survival that exists intrinsically within them), their animal-ego selves will naturally doom them to operate at a level that will preclude them from the fresh start and freedom from suffering that being "born again" promises.

Using the Christian reference once again, it was said that "the Kingdom of Heaven is within you." What does that mean? Could it mean that the peace, joy, purpose, and fulfillment that is possible in the human condition and that represents various states of heaven that we associate with it are actually available to us by transitioning to a larger identity? Our Level 4 Identity perhaps?

I can give you countless examples of the truth of this premise. I have literally had 18,000 hours over the last eighteen years of intense, personal, deep coaching conversations with clients who consistently confirm the truth of this empowerment. Additionally, I have the example of all of the members of my original family in this life. All of those conversations, as well as the examples of my family, do nothing but verify and validate this great truth: moving from Level 3 to Level 4 is the key to what we are all seeking.

VALIDATING THE GREAT TRUTH

Let me share a couple of examples.

I'll start with my mother. Ruth was born in 1920 in Ohio. The youngest of three sisters, she always felt like the ugly duckling. She was a sweet woman who wanted to be a good human being, but her neuroses and anxieties and insecurities precluded her from optimizing happiness in life. By the time I met her, she was (of course) the only mother example I've ever had. My experience of her while I was growing up was that she was overweight, a chain smoker (three packs a day for fifty years), an alcoholic, a gambling addict, and afraid of seemingly everything. Her neuroses took the form of constant worrying and doting on every thought or action that I seem to have had as a child and a teenager. Her fears included cats, mountains, fire, and other people thinking ill of her. When we would leave the house before going for a drive in the 1950s and 1960s, she would make us go through the house and gather all of the ashtrays and put them in the bathtub so fire couldn't magically leap out and burn the house down.

If I'm honest, I became disappointed in her as I entered into my teen years. I am ashamed to say, I probably was ashamed of her for being so weak and anxious and neurotic, despite her clear intentionality to be a loving mother.

She simply didn't know how to be an effectively loving mother. Why? Because she was still, in effect, the same neurotic fourteen-year-old she had been in 1934 until her death at age seventy-six. She was my first experience in the dark side of Level 3 Identity. Perhaps she was part of the existential awareness that grew in me with each passing year that, despite our best desires and intentions, if we don't learn how to control our minds, our ability to present our best selves to the world is sabotaged—along with our fulfillment in life for ourselves.

But did these effects on me truly, objectively, capture who my mom was? No. She did have a Level 4. But I was largely blind to it.

My mom's Level 4 showed up in her early nurturing of me and my siblings (the long, sleepless nights with sick children, holding scared hands approaching the kindergarten door of life, the quiet selflessness of protecting us from harm). She demonstrated love, selflessness, and kindness to me constantly, but it was overridden over time by her Level 3 habits and scripting.

Her values ultimately surrendered to her ego—her love submitted to her fear.

What about my older sister? Like my mother, she was a sweet person with a good heart, but had all of the same demons of my mother. She was just a younger version of the same.

As a result of her response to her distrust of life born out of her Level 3 Identity, she ran away from home when I was ten years old (she was seventeen) and got married and moved away to New York City. I subsequently only saw her four times until her death at age seventy-one. We never really had a relationship.

What about her Level 4? Did it ever show up? Of course. It shows up for all of us now and then. She was a selfless mother when her neuroses didn't interrupt it, a loving wife, courageous survivor of life challenges, and warm-hearted member of her community in Brooklyn. But, again, as with my mom, her fretful interaction with life and fear ultimately had her succumb to a life of self-indulgent addictive habits that shortened and lessened what life could have been for her.

What about my older brother? He was my best friend growing up. Three years older than I, he guided me (or at least tried to) through the travails of being a young teenage boy in the late 1960s. He told me how to get girls. He told me how to make friends. He told me how to see life. And he taught me how to drink alcohol.

As I continued my growth, education, and business success, he went a different direction. For him, he peaked in high school and the party never stopped, or at least he didn't want it to. Accordingly, he went through two marriages and three careers before finally succumbing to advanced alcoholism in his early forties. For the last fifteen years of his life, he was a dangerous homeless person who threatened my parents and me through his downward spiral of alcoholism. I actually had to protect my parents from him, even to the point of getting a concealed carry permit in my forties to make sure that any potential violence he brought to the family could hopefully be thwarted.

The last time I saw him, I almost hit him with my car while I was driving down the street in Boulder. He stepped off the curb in a drunken haze at ten o'clock in the morning, and I had to swerve to avoid him. I recognized him, but he no longer recognized me. He was too lost in the catacombs of his own drunken haze and spiraling addiction to alcohol. As I drove on past him in my expensive German luxury automobile, the irony of life couldn't be escaped.

Here was my closest confidant and friend and family member who no longer recognized me from four feet away, and I didn't dare recognize him at the risk of his seeking my home out, along with all that risk. I had spent decades trying to rescue him from himself, but we all must, ultimately, rescue ourselves. And the only way I know to do that is through our elevation to Level 4 consciousness, which is our personal responsibility.

Others who love us may help, support, and educate us, but in the end, the results of our lives are going to be a reflection of our own actions in response to what life presents to us. And those actions are going to come from how poorly or how masterfully we discipline our minds, which reflects what level of identity we are operating from at each moment.

When the three bureaucrats from the Boulder County Coroner's Department came to my house one night to tell me my brother had died in the streets, I'm ashamed to admit that I felt nothing, except perhaps relief. The great drama of watching my older brother spiral down into his own personal hell and try to drag us with it was finally over.

But I remember his Level 4 well, simultaneously. When I quit my job one time and only had a few hundred dollars in the bank and was scared to death, he was there reassuring me that my future was still bright. When a bully would threaten me at school, he was there to defend me.

Yet, he, too, ultimately succumbed to his lesser Self and died prematurely with a life that could have been so much more.

Finally, my father. While my mother, sister, and brother demonstrated with their life habits and experiences the dangers and emptiness of living life in Level 3, my father gave me an overt glimpse of Level 4.

My father was born in Troy, New York, in 1913. Raised with six brothers and sisters in a poor, Irish, Catholic household, his mother died when he was five years old giving birth. His father died one month later from "a broken heart" (that is code among the Irish for alcoholism).

My father was shipped off to an orphanage in 1919. Most of his siblings were sent to different orphanages, so he was all but alone at six years old. He was reportedly treated very harshly in the orphanage. In those years, the brothers and the nuns of the Catholic religion believed in tough love. So he was often beaten, among other abuses.

When my father finally escaped the orphanage, he was eighteen. What was happening in 1931? The Great Depression was visited upon America. What was a young man fresh out of the orphanage to do in a country and a world where there were no jobs available, yet he had to survive somehow?

What he chose to do was go to work in the government at a job that his uncle got him out of the Democratic political machine in New York. He never liked the job, despite spending the next forty years doing it. He found the bureaucratic systems and the mediocrity of intentionality and effectiveness deeply offensive to his personal moral code.

So what did he do? He decided to operate as a man of principle and integrity and effectiveness, despite the system and those people around him who resented him for caring so much. I watched that noble man live his whole life paycheck to paycheck, never owning a house, and his most prized possession being a used Chevrolet. He never complained. Quite the opposite. He was forever upbeat and happy and supportive and loving to everyone around him.

He humbly went about his life showing an expression of principled behavior applied through a personality of selfless integrity. As a result, he died at ninety-five years of age, having been a widower for twelve years after his wife (my mom) passed away. Even when she died, after he called to ask me to come to Las Vegas (where they lived) and help with my mom's death, he had called the authorities and cleaned it all up and made it sanitary and safe for me to come and try to help him and not have to go through the grief that he surely did. He had taken care of his wife's body who had died in the night in an alcoholic haze, only to have him find her in the morning.

He undoubtedly felt great grief for having lost his life partner of fifty years of marriage, but I never would have known it. Even amid his unbearable grief, he made me feel as if it was all taken care of and I only needed to process my own grief. He was his Level 4 for me even as his Level 3 was undoubtedly in agony, demonstrating a courage of love that I can't imagine.

My father taught me essentially the same principle that Viktor Frankl shares in his landmark book *Man's Search for Meaning*—that principle being that whatever happens to you in life, you always retain the power to look at it in whatever way you choose to, and the more nobly you choose to look at it, the greater your power within it.

My father taught me honor, humility, and integrity.

He further taught me how to operate with the intentionality and support for what's best for others, despite how dysfunctional they may be. That became true selflessness to me, and through his example, I was taught the invaluable principles that led to a forty-five-year search and gathering of information that is summarized in the principles of this book.

THE STORY OF SIDDHARTHA

This dynamic of living in our Level 3 ego-based Self is predominant and commonplace in the world. It creates the majority of our suffering. It limits our power. It precludes our hope. And it invites self-diminishment and self-doubt, which undermines our ability to realize our fullest potential. It is the historic triumph of selfish egocentrism of the animal within us over the angelic and divine portion of us that reflects our Source. That is Level 3 life.

Some 2,500 years ago, for example, there lived a rich kid in India named Siddhartha. His father was a big deal and owned a great estate, and he went out of his way to make sure that Siddhartha had a positive experience of life on the material plane. But even after a life of privilege, Siddhartha realized that old age, sickness, and death would eventually come to all of us.

With this realization, Siddhartha could no longer enjoy his life of relative comfort compared to those around him, because, in the end, suffering would be his eventual destiny as well, along with everyone he knew and loved. That was unacceptable to him. After all, how could he enjoy the peace of today if he knew that tomorrow would bring incredible suffering to him and everyone he loved?

Accordingly, he went out in search of the answer. Without detailing what his process was, he essentially went through his awakening where he revealed to the world his formula for escaping the cycle of suffering. In essence, at least as I interpret it, he concluded that the source of suffering is the tendency to attach to things that are ever in change, impermanent, and treat them as though they are permanent.

The vehicle for this attachment is the ego, according to the Buddha (which became his identity instead of Siddhartha, and means "The Awakened One"). Because the ego wants to survive, it tries to make everything around it permanent so that it can define its place relative to the experiences in the world, and desperately tries to make permanent that which is not. But life is moving ever forward in its evolution, and that means growth, and growth means change, and change means impermanence of the apparently permanent.

I believe what Buddha was talking about is the need to move from Level 3 Identity (ego) to Level 4 Identity, which operates from a place beyond this need to create permanence out of the impermanent.

Approximately 500 years after the Buddha came Jesus of Nazareth. Among other things, what was one of his key messages? Throughout the New Testament Jesus repeatedly taught his disciples and the people around him that they must "die to themselves." This has been interpreted through most Christian sects as meaning that they must follow a particular protocol that their particular sect emphasizes, whether that be a methodology to personal salvation, being born again, being baptized, being a Catholic, or some other interpretation.

Is it possible to interpret the words of Christ in a different, more open and universal fashion? I believe so. I believe what he was saying is that the Self we must die to is Level 3, ego-based identity. When we "die" to this Self, and we assume a larger identity beyond the unchallenged and often unconscious rules of ego-based identity, we enter into a new paradigm and relationship with reality through a transformation of our own identity.

In another example from the Christian path, is it possible that when Christ declared, "When two or more are gathered in my name, I shall be there," he meant something different than is commonly interpreted? Perhaps because Christ was love personified as his Level 4 (or, in his case, perhaps even some levels beyond that), he was saying, "When two or more are gathered in the name of love, I am there!"

Why? Perhaps because when we gather in love, we *are* love—love is present—and it invites that state to others present. It is eternal and omnipresent in a timeless oneness with others where there is no separation between us, and there is no time, no past, no future, just the now, and that now is eternity at that moment. We are complete.

Perhaps God is simply love. Perhaps love is what created the universe and is our connection point to eternity, and when we pass from this physical existence, we merge into the ocean of love from which we came. Perhaps the religions of the world have interpreted that through the lens of the level of consciousness predominant when they were formed, which would naturally tend to anthropomorphize the message into a particular individual in history, a set of dogmatic rules, a defined belief system that, if you don't endorse it, you may be deemed blasphemous or worse.

Perhaps this is the essence of dogma in all forms: the separation of my belief from those who don't agree and are therefore wrong. Perhaps dogma is simply Level 3 conscripting the essential and universal message of love-based oneness and making it a pathology to be worshiped and defended with the vitriol of "me" fighting with "the other."

The Buddhists have a beautiful description of this process when they say, "Don't confuse the finger pointing at the moon… as the moon."

After all, is the point of religion to realize the truth of spirituality (the intrinsic unity of all of existence), or is spirituality simply something being sought through the vehicle of religion for those who are attracted to that path? Are we pursuing our spirit walk as Level 3 or as Level 4?

Are we confusing the messenger with the message?

A MESSAGE OF PERSONAL SALVATION

This pathway is available to all people, even if they've never been exposed to the teachings of Christ. In other words, personal salvation may mean something different from, or in addition to, the traditional interpretations of salvation.

In the context of this exploration, salvation may mean saving yourself from the limited, intrinsically suffering, and temporary existence as an ego while in this dimension of reality called human existence. This seems like an overwhelming task to most human beings. It seems farcical, philosophical, impractical, impossible, or debatable. Is there ever any way out of this conundrum that is the cycle of suffering that is intrinsic to an ego-based identity, regardless of how materially comfortable you may be at this moment? What if there is no hope? And, actually, how can there ever truly be hope when old age, sickness, and death await us all if we believe that we are merely our Level 3 egos with our temporary lives as such?

But there is hope for this dynamic that is so commonplace in all of our lives. In fact, there is more than hope. There is a way out of the conundrum of mediocrity, and the pendulum of happiness to sadness back to sadness to happiness. The fundamental opportunity of discovering, awakening, learning, and practicing a Level 4 Identity-guided life is the evolution beyond the karmic and predictable challenges of everyday life that create the distress and emptiness that most of us feel too much of the time as adults.

And the implications are even greater than that. Living in your Level 4 Identity will create freedom for you that makes you eligible for the power to impact your life in profound ways beyond what you can imagine.

Whatever you believe God is (if you believe He exists at all), or the Source, the Universe, Yahweh, Divinity, or the Tao—whatever you believe that macro-intelligence behind it all is—that entity can now trust you with the power to manifest a future that fulfills you and empowers you to live to your fullest potential.

Absolutely

Without question

Every time

Because you can now be trusted with such power, since you are doing it from a greater level of identity that goes beyond mere self-interest and self-promotion (ego). You are now an expression of that Universal Source of all that is, consciously, by personifying the values that are the connecting force among all things.

I promise.

PROOF OF LEVEL 4 IDENTITY

Many amazing transformations occur when a person operates from their Level 4 versus their Level 3 selves. And many of these transformations dissolve the very sources of suffering that are so constant for people living at Level 3. What are some of those transformations that take place when you choose to live as a personification of your values?

- The outside-to-in relationship with life experienced at Level 3 is instantly reversed to an inside-to-out relationship with life. The Level 4 person has the power to create what they want. Because what he or she wants will now be worth creating beyond mere self-gratification on behalf of the individual self-interest within us all, and the Universe responds with trust by empowering that Level 4 individual with the ability to awaken the same state in others—and accomplish miraculous feats.

- The trunk of evidence that gets ever larger within Level 3 Identity, and creates the emptiness in our soul as we age, is now eliminated out of your life. Because Level 4 Self is no longer a separate, self-serving identity grounded in ego as at Level 3, there is no longer the ego-based dynamic of constant self-judgment. The eradication of self-judgment eliminates the conditional love the Level 3 person is only capable of experiencing with himself or herself, because there is not a ledger of sin and guilt versus good actions and intentions. There is no longer a need to keep a report card on shame and mediocrity and mistakes. Because they no longer matter.

What matters now is your intentionality toward the world and yourself in a future that is no longer hobbled by the past, even though it has learned from the past how to get better. Why? Because you lead the process of your thoughts and actions through your intentions, and if your intentions are now grounded in being a reflection of your core values, a force of light, a force for good, your thoughts and actions will reflect those intentions and manifest accordingly.

- The power of manifestation is the third major transformation that occurs in moving from Level 3 to Level 4 existence. A person living at Level 4 is operating as an expression of values. Values are the language of Divinity on the planet that we all share. Such values as love, compassion, humility, faith, truthfulness, selflessness, sacrifice, wisdom, and gratitude are all positively recognized by humanity as being the ultimate guidelines for human activity. When a person operates as a personification of one or more of these, they create a predictable response from whomever they interact with that is a reflection of those values.

If all of the above is true, we should have many, many examples in history of the truth of Level 4 human existence. Let's look at a few of the high-water marks of humanity that may validate the premise of Level 4 Identity:

- Jesus Christ: We don't know much about his personality, but when I ask people what values he personified, they consistently list qualities such as love, forgiveness, and sacrifice.

- Buddha: What values did Buddha personify? Compassion, mindfulness, wisdom, inner peace.

- Gandhi: Truthfulness, courage, humility, nonviolence.

- Mother (now Saint) Teresa: Unconditional love for everyone regardless of their station in life, service, and humility.

- Martin Luther King: Equality, social justice, courage.

- St. Francis: Humility, love.

What about historical figures that we don't normally think of as spiritual figures? Imagine yourself in 1944 living in the largest city in the world, which is London, and 60 percent of the 7 million people who live there have to live underground in the subways because the Nazis are bombing the city, which is on fire. Mothers are breastfeeding babies in the dark catacombs of the subways; dust is falling; children are crying; and Londoners fear that next rocket or bomb may hit them.

Over the radio, a gravelly voice says this: "A thousand years from now, people will say this is the moment good fought back evil. Never, never, never give up!" Winston Churchill represented courage, patriotism, and effectiveness.

John F. Kennedy gave two speeches declaring that America would have a man on the moon by the end of the decade of the 1960s. His intention was to demonstrate the superiority of a freedom-based society compared to the government-controlled society of the Soviet Union. He gave two speeches on the subject before he was tragically assassinated. But because he was so passionate and effective and personifying courage, vision, and resolve, other people made his vision come true even after he died. He, accordingly, represented vision, passion, and patriotism.

Generous gifts from the Bill & Melinda Gates Foundation relieve millions of people from suffering by utilizing the resources that Bill Gates created with Microsoft and his resulting wealth to help people experience compassion, hope, and health.

And, last, here's an experience that you have probably gone through personally. If you look at a typical family in the world, you see the parents practicing Level 4 Identity toward their children in their better moments of parenting. I think this is not an accident. I think the powerful but subtle truth of Level 4 Identity is built into the architecture of being a human being by Divinity to help give us an experience of what Level 4 feels like. A mother selflessly stays up with her child when he's sick as a baby, even though she's dead tired and wants to sleep. Why? Love! Selflessness! Compassion! A father works eighteen-hour days and three jobs to make sure that his family has enough to eat, but makes sure to show up at his daughter's piano recital even though she's only in the fifth grade and doesn't play all that great. Sacrifice, discipline, resolve, creativity, stewardship.

Proof of Level 4 Identity is all around us. It comes to us, I believe, through everyday experiences in the interface of human beings with one another. But because we haven't defined it, and therefore systematized an access point to *being it* more often, it comes and goes as a transitory state. When one consciously awakens the decision to live from Level 4 more and more often in their life, life responds like a mirror and begins to give the person making that decision a profound life of fulfillment unavailable at a lower level of identity.

What I am about to say to you will strike you as either blasphemous, ridiculous, or the most profound truth that you may have ever heard, but here it is: When you operate at Level 4, you operate as a reflection of the light and power of Divinity, and therefore have much of that same power to create a future unlimited by your past—a future that fulfills your life destiny and eliminates the void within you.

If you read that statement and consider it possible, your Level 4 is resonating with it and, in worldly terms, you are resonating with your spirituality.

If you read that and recoil in judgment, harshness, or offense, your Level 3 dogma is protecting an expansion of your paradigm of beliefs from the so-called threat that you don't already have all the answers, and you have more work to do. You may consider that a sign of being religious or atheistic or whatever, rather than focusing on your spirituality.

Level 4 Identity allows human existence to finally make sense beyond the typical pathology of merely seeking pleasure and survival until we die, as well as how to avoid the need from Level 3 to see anyone or anything as a threat to us who don't agree with what our current beliefs are, and is therefore a threat that has to be judged or fought.

That isn't the real, ultimate version of you that is fighting it. It is simply the ego within you trying to convince you that all you are is your Level 3, your ego. It is simply your Level 3 being expressed as dogma, and that limited identity is what creates the majority of human-related suffering on the planet. And this whole dynamic is part of the spiritual awakening process to see the bankruptcy of dogma as something to be grown past, to be neutralized through an expansion of understanding. Level 4 Identity only feels threatening to our ego (Level 3), and it is our ego that is whispering to us that Level 4 is dangerous, wrong, or even sinful to think such things.

POP QUIZ

Who are some people in your life who personally gave you an experience of unconditional love, an experience of compassion, of generosity, of gratitude, or any other Level 4 value? What impact did it have on your life? Put your insights in your journal please.

5

HOW TO AWAKEN AND LIVE YOUR LEVEL 4 IDENTITY

To change one's life:

Start immediately

Do it flamboyantly

No exceptions

No excuses.

—William James

Level 4 Identity is available to all human beings with normal functioning mental hardware and software. In other words, it may or may not be available to people who have limited mental function, for whatever reason. But the vast majority of human beings, regardless of religion, culture, gender, race, and ethnicity can practice the awakening and living from this dramatically more empowered Self.

But how do we actually get there? How do we awaken our Level 4 Identity and then go on to live from that identity to enjoy the results promised by doing so?

The first step is to become aware that Level 4 Identity even exists. You are reading this book to become aware of this concept and then to try it on to see if what I'm saying could possibly be true, right? Understanding and living at Level 4 is not without its challenges. Let's explore how to awaken your Level 4 Identity, develop a habit of practicing your life from that identity, and then notice the experiences and results from doing so.

AWAKENING YOUR LEVEL 4 IDENTITY

When asked by a follower if he was a God,
the Buddha simply replied:
"I am Awake."

Not living a "Level 4" life was a void I felt from within but did not have the tools or awareness to identify. *Through recognizing the personal vision by which I want to exist I am equipped with a new filter to view life.* **The desire to serve something greater than myself has enriched my relationship with God, my family, and the fulfillment of my career.**

—*Adam Fleming*
Husband/Father/Business Owner

The steps

- Awareness

- Decision

- Personal Life Vision (PLV) Creation

- Personal Life Vision, Level 4 Identity Experience

- Assess and Adjust to Grow

To awaken your Level 4 Identity requires the very critical first step of being aware that this level even exists. Without this first step, you will never be able to access your Level 4 Identity unless you stumble upon it as few human beings ever have. Or you will periodically practice it without differentiating it from your everyday mind (Level 3), and therefore it will come and go without your conscious awareness of it.

Awareness means that you must cognitively recognize that you probably aren't living at your highest level of identity if you are a typical human being, even as an adult, because you are really just practicing your Level 3 Identity at a more advanced level. That advanced level means that you are still subject to many of the scripts and experiences of middle school or early adolescence, but have learned through life experiences subsequent to that period of your life how to be more effective and subtle within that same level of identity.

In other words, when we operate as an ego that is physically mature, life experiences refine our ability to react to situations so that the glaring consequences from inappropriate action become less glaring as we age. We get better at deceiving ourselves that our ego is serving our life purpose. This happens because we confuse the lower levels of Maslow's hierarchy of needs (basics for survival such as food and water, psychological needs such as social acceptance) as proof that our ego identity is serving us as we grow more secure in our survival with time.

Typically we do grow more secure with time as we age as adults, at least as measured by our ability to survive. This happens because we typically build our economics to where we become more independent and have more options for more experiences through wealth creation and the freedom from worry that such perceived security provides us.

Since we define having more experiences as being synonymous with living a bigger and more purposeful life, we begin to pursue material acquisition and travel and stimulating experiences that interest us as proof that our life is fulfilling.

But this is deception of the Self. Because, while we are more comfortable and we feel "safer," we are not necessarily more fulfilled on the inside at a deep level of need to be significant. In fact, we often forget significance altogether until life forces us to remember it. We often think that our so-called success represents proof that we are living the best life possible.

But once we have a life scare, that life scare frightens us into recognizing that we may not have the capabilities that will be required to endure the changes in life, up to and including the death of our loved ones, health problems, or even our own physical death.

Life scare is a term that can represent anything from a child on drugs, a divorce, a health trauma, a job loss, or any number of life challenges that can take us back down to the place of insecurity and fear. Once we are in that state, paralyzed with fear and uncertain of what to do next, we often only then recognize the "hole in our soul" that has been there all along and that we have not noticed because of our distraction with comfort. This may well be what creates middle-age crazy for many people.

Decision represents the second step in awakening your Level 4 Identity. Decision represents the conscious choice to change the pattern of your life. You will do this either the easy way or the hard way. The easy way is to learn from other people who know how to do it in practice by what they have realized through that experience without having to go through that experience yourself. The hard way is to ignore the experience and teachings of others, often out of the arrogance of ego being a knower, and waiting until some traumatic event occurs in your life that forces you to look at a new way forward.

Either way, a decision must be made for a change. The overwhelming majority of people never even become aware that a higher level of identity even exists. But even of those who are aware, many lack the boldness, courage, or pathology to make the decision that they are capable of change. So the decision step requires personal courage. And it is awakening that courageous choice of a new path forward that in itself represents the first major breakthrough for awakening your Level 4 once you are aware that it exists.

Once the decision has been made, you will naturally know what to do next, which sets up the next step in the process: creating your own **Personal Life Vision** (PLV):

Personal Life Vision looks inward and becomes life purpose;
Personal Life Vision looks outward and becomes life aspiration;
Personal Life Vision looks upward and becomes life Faith.

The next step in the process is to create your own North Star, your own reason to be, your own Personal Life Vision. There is a very specific process to follow for awakening a Personal Life Vision. You will know how to do that in a moment, but first I need to define what a Personal Life Vision is.

A Personal Life Vision is one of the most important, powerful, and sacred gifts to yourself and others that you can create and practice in your life. It is your personal commitment to the future that you are making on behalf of an identity and a group larger than merely your own personal self-interest. It is a conscious creation of the legacy of your life. This is what you hope others remember most about you at your funeral. It is a guidance system of filters through which you can make decisions that you can trust. It is rooted in your personal life values, which are the indicators within you of your greater life purpose and pathology. It is a sacred covenant with God/Divinity/the Source that you willingly hold yourself accountable to—being the very best version of yourself that you could possibly be while in the human physical dimension. It is also, through its practice, what earns you the trustworthiness for power to impact others in this life and, through doing so, fulfills your soul at all levels and in all ways regardless of how comfortable or uncomfortable your life. It is the "keys to the kingdom" for accessing that place of deep peace in fulfillment and acceptance and love within you that you quietly crave, yet so consistently evades you when living at Level 3.

The PLV is a statement that you create that declares your highest purpose toward the future. There is a specific and systematic way to create a PLV, and everyone can do it. Many people feel incapable of creating such a sacred and noble commitment and feel insecure about finding the right words to say it perfectly. If you feel this way as you begin this process, that is totally understandable. But you need not fear the process, because I promise it works if you simply follow the steps. Remember, it is not about the statement anyway, or how beautifully it is articulated, or what others will say about it, or even being a perfect expression of your commitment to your core values. In the end, the ultimate value of your PLV is the sincerity with which you apply it in your life. If you do that, the aesthetic of how well or inspirationally it is articulated pales in importance.

To look at it correctly, remember: your Personal Life Vision is a declaration of your heart to the world, not your head, your ego, your image, or how others react to it.

It is not you in the common meaning of the term. It is your Soul. It is the Universe talking through you. It is the Divinity within you. So trust it, however pretty the words declaring it sound.

To create your PLV, use the following tools.

PERSONAL CORE VALUES

Step 1: From the list of core values on the following pages, place a check mark next to the top twenty values most important to you. This is merely a starting list of possible values that may capture your personal core values, or it may be incomplete. That is fine. Simply add whatever value or values to the list before starting to check off your top twenty.

For example, you may really resonate with *gratitude*, and that value is not on the list. Simply write *gratitude* on the bottom of one of the columns of values before you begin your process of choosing and distilling the values.

Step 2: From the list of twenty core values checked, circle the ten most important values to you. Don't feel like you are giving up on the ten you didn't choose at this step; you are simply picking the biggest ten. In fact, try to correlate the ones you didn't keep into the ones that you did.

For example, if you added the value *honor* to the overall list before you began and chose it as one of your top twenty, and you also chose *integrity* from the beginning list, you may keep *integrity* and leave *honor* off the top ten list because you believe that *honor* is a part of *integrity* already. You may believe that *integrity* is a larger, more significant value than *honor*, and that *honor* is a part of *integrity* anyway, so you aren't leaving *honor* behind by choosing the value of *integrity*.

Step 3: Choose your top three core values from those ten, and write them on the page following the list of core values and answer the questions about each value.

CORE VALUES

_____	Achievement	_____	Knowledge
_____	Advancement and promotion	_____	Leadership
_____	Adventure	_____	Location
_____	Affection (love and caring)	_____	Loyalty
_____	Arts	_____	Market position
_____	Challenging problems	_____	Meaningful work
_____	Change and variety	_____	Merit
_____	Charity	_____	Money
_____	Close relationships	_____	Nature
_____	Community	_____	Being around people who are
_____	Compassion		open and honest
_____	Competence	_____	Order (tranquility, stability,
_____	Competition		conformity)
_____	Cooperation	_____	Personal development (living up
_____	Country		to the fullest use of my potential)
_____	Creativity	_____	Physical challenge
_____	Decisiveness	_____	Pleasure
_____	Democracy	_____	Power and authority
_____	Ecological awareness	_____	Privacy
_____	Economic security	_____	Public service
_____	Effectiveness	_____	Purity
_____	Efficiency	_____	Quality of what I take part in
_____	Ethical practice	_____	Quality relationships
_____	Excellence	_____	Recognition
_____	Excitement	_____	Respect from others
_____	Expertise	_____	Religion
_____	Faith	_____	Reputation
_____	Fame	_____	Responsibility and accountability
_____	Fast living	_____	Security
_____	Fast-paced work	_____	Self-respect
_____	Fidelity	_____	Serenity
_____	Financial gain	_____	Service to others
_____	Freedom	_____	Sophistication
_____	Friendships	_____	Spirituality
_____	Growth	_____	Stability
_____	Having a family	_____	Status
_____	Helping other people	_____	Supervising others
_____	Helping society	_____	Time freedom
_____	Honesty	_____	Trust
_____	Independence	_____	Truth
_____	Influencing others	_____	Wealth
_____	Inner harmony	_____	Wisdom
_____	Integrity	_____	Work under pressure
_____	Intellectual status	_____	Work with others
_____	Involvement	_____	Working alone
_____	Job tranquility		

EMPOWERING PERSONAL CORE VALUES

With regard to each of your three core values, please answer the following:

VALUE #1: _____

How do you personally define this value?

What would your life and the world be like if this value were more prominent and practiced?

Are you willing to commit to a life where this value is paramount?

VALUE #2: _____

How do you define this value?

What would your life and the world be like if this value were more prominent and practiced?

Are you willing to commit to a life where this value is paramount?

VALUE #3: _____

How do you define this value?

What would your life and the world be like if this value were more prominent and practiced?

Are you willing to commit to a life where this value is paramount?

PERSONAL LIFE VISION STATEMENT

1. Review your answers about your three core values and your commitment to make them paramount in your life.

2. Amplify your commitment to practicing those values as an act of amplifying your life legacy and fulfillment, using your desire to live a greater life.

3. Create a statement that represents your commitment for the future:

   ☐ The statement should be long enough to include your commitment, yet brief enough to recall without notes.

   ☐ The statement should describe the current reality in the future (for example, "A world that treats all people with love, compassion and integrity" (present tense)).

   ☐ The more inclusive the statement, the more power the statement will have. (Start it with "My Personal Life Vision is a world or a community or a place—," and it will be more inclusive and powerful than if merely about you and your immediate family or smaller group.)

   ☐ The more specific the statement, the more focused the power will be. (Use your three core values to be focused with your commitment.)

   ☐ Your statement is not personal; it is not only about you. It describes future conditions that include you along with a larger group you are a part of, up to and including all people.

   ☐ Try multiple versions using either a formula or clause-based approach and then pick the one that most inspires your commitment, and therefore your heart and passion.

   Formula example: "My Personal Life Vision is a world where all people experience love through compassion and integrity."

Clause-based approach: "My Personal Life Vision is a world where:

>...all people practice integrity;
>
>...all intentions are based in compassion;
>
>...all people experience unconditional love constantly."

Write your Personal Life Vision statement now.

Here are some examples that may help you get started:

"My Personal Life Vision is a World where all people realize love, peace, and prosperity through helping others do so."

—Your Name

"My Personal Life Vision is a Community where...
—Integrity is the foundation of all
   decisions and actions;
—Truth is the ever-present guidance
   behind all interface;
—Family love is experienced by all."

—Your Name

"My Personal Life Vision is a Place where compassion is consistently practiced as the highest form of love, and all beings are blessed by inner peace as a result."

—Your Name

Let's move to the next step: Personal Life Vision, Level 4 Identity **experience.**

Values are the language Divinity uses to communicate with our hearts.

Once you've created a PLV, you must now bring it to life. In my first book, *Soul Proprietorship: 8 Critical Steps to Overcoming Problems in Business and Life*, I shared a formula for the ownership of truth. This formula is C + E = OT. This stands for concept plus experience equals the ownership of truth.

For us to actually "own" truth, we must do more than just entertain it as a belief. Concept without experience is merely theory. Experience without concept is not repeatable upon command or trainable as a tool of empowerment. But if you put the two of them together, they help you really know things as your own so that you both know how they work as well as how to do them. They are no longer mere intellectual theories or beliefs, but actually part of your body of knowledge you may call upon without question.

You may remember being a little child moving from a three-wheel tricycle to a two-wheel bike. Your parent might've told you how the two wheels would be safe and wouldn't fall over as long as you pedal the bicycle. This was the concept of gyroscopic motion that your parent taught you so that your belief in your ability to ride a two-wheel bicycle was enhanced. But you had to get on the bike and have your dad, or your mom, hold onto the seat as you rode down the street the first time. Remember that moment? You, pedaling along and staying up instead of falling over, and you call back, "You can let go now, Daddy," or "You can let go now, Mommy," thinking that they were still holding you up.

Only then did you realize that they had let go a hundred yards earlier and you have been riding the bicycle all by yourself. And you have never forgotten how to do so since. The concept of riding the bicycle plus the experience of actually doing it meant that you would never again be ignorant of how to ride a bicycle. And you can now teach others how to do so because you understand the concept of it.

Creating and experiencing a PLV is exactly the same process. This book introduces you to the concept of why you should have such a vision. But you must "ride the bicycle" or, in other words, practice that personalized vision through your decisions in life to begin to own its power.

But exactly how do you do this? How do you consciously change your identity to something new and different that is not only real, but can end up feeling more real than the reality you believed to be singularly true thus far in life?

It best begins by doing what was first on the list in creating a PLV and is also first on the list to experiencing it as the access point to your Level 4 Identity most easily: awareness.

One must maintain a constant awareness of his or her PLV to be able to experience Level 4 Identity intentionally. There are other ways to experience Level 4, but they don't tend to be as intentional or guided as when accessed through a remembrance of your PLV. There will be times, for example, when you find yourself moved to help an old lady across the street. Or perhaps to help a young child who's fallen on the playground, to lift her up and dust off her bloodied knee and comfort her. These are but a few of countless examples where we operate as our Level 4 Identity, but these experiences tend to be hit or miss and dependent upon our state of mind at the moment.

The reason that a PLV is such a consistent and constant access point to our Level 4 Identity is that it moves belief in something to a commitment to act upon that belief. It is a decision point through which you choose to filter your reality in your thoughts, impressions, intentions, and reactions.

Once you begin to practice and experience some regular awareness of your PLV, it now becomes a tool, a filter through which you can process experiences. This is very empowering if used properly. Shall we look at some examples?

OSCILLATION IN APPLICATION TO LIFE DOMAINS

●————————————————————————————————●

Success is not final,
failure is not fatal:
it is the courage to continue that counts.
—*Winston Churchill*

Desire, anger and delusion are negative forces,

but they also represent the energy and majesty of the Buddha-nature in its elemental state;

The practice of Buddhism is concerned with becoming aware of these passions and calming them until they are transformed into joy, warmth, generosity, energy and wisdom.

Once familiar with these forces, we can work with and transform them...

—*His Holiness The 14th Dalai Lama*

I was driving home from work the other night after a long day. It was one of those moments in traffic that we all face now and then. Bumper to bumper, honking horns, people anxious to get home to their families. I was driving along at 45 miles an hour, and I noticed a woman come up behind me and sit closely off my rear bumper at the same speed. Within a few moments she rapidly shifted over to the right-hand lane and pulled up next to me. She was now riding the bumper of the person in front of her in her lane. I could tell that she was in a tremendous hurry, and that her driving seemed erratic as a result of her impatience.

Some intuition occurred within me that I should be very leery of her next actions. It is, after all, not that uncommon for people in this sort of situation to suddenly pull into your lane without letting you know. So I backed off a little bit so that I would have time to stop if she swerved into my lane. Sure enough, she just charged over into my lane without so much as a second thought, much less a turn signal. She almost hit my front bumper, and I honked my horn angrily. She remained indifferent or aloof or unconscious and simply kept driving chatting with the woman next to her in the seat.

This is a classic moment that would invite my Level 3 anger, a major personality element within me that has been one of my worst features my whole life. I have a habit of getting angry whenever something surprising happens, I guess because I naturally assume that it could've been prevented and somebody simply didn't care enough to do so—whatever the situation.

Well, in this case, my first reaction was to sit on her bumper at 45 miles an hour and glare at her and, if she looked at me, make an obscene gesture with my right middle finger. My Level 3 was raging at how delicious it would be to pay her back. I was allowing my mind to run with thoughts like "who does that bitch think she is?" Or even "I should run her off the road, pull her out of the car, and beat the crap out of her!"

My anger and self-righteousness and potential violence were completely understandable given the "tapes" I was playing in my mind. I am ashamed to admit, there have been too many times in my life where I have listened to that voice of anger and righteous indignation and taken actions that have later come to cost me dearly. I'm sure the sort of situation happens regularly to people in America with busy lives who have a great degree of responsibilities and desire to get it all done. Nevertheless, there was a quiet decision point that I knew was present in my mind as I rode in the car eighteen inches off her back bumper.

I consciously recognized that I had a choice in this moment: I could follow through on the delicious anger my mind was fueling, or I could look at her and the situation through my Level 4. What would happen if I acted out of my Level 3 impulse? Legal consequences? Economic consequences? Health or even life survival consequences, if she had a gun or something? My anger didn't care. My self-righteousness didn't care. The tapes played in my mind at loud volume that I needed to show her who was boss, to teach her a lesson.

However, thank God, I also had another part of me watching it all unfold. That part of me may be called the witness. The witness that resides within us simply observes the experiences of our life without the need to judge them or comment on them. It is that part of us that simply observes what's occurring and watches our response to what's occurring. It doesn't weigh in with judgments, moralities, opinions, or any other sort of qualifier. It simply is aware.

Out of that state of awareness from the witness within me, I consciously recognized I had a choice at that moment: to be either my Level 3 or my Level 4. I quickly realized that my Level 3 would feel great in the moment, or at least so I thought. But clearly it had all sorts of implications that could end up making me suffer even more than my current indignation. I simultaneously recognized that my Level 4 would create a response that would have no karmic consequences.

So I asked myself what my PLV was. And I reminded myself that my PLV is a commitment to be a force in the world where all people realize their fullest potential, experience extraordinary relationships and extraordinary accomplishments, and both practice and experience integrity and honorable actions courageously in their interface with the world.

As I remembered and I replaced my Level 3 tapes of righteous indignation with the values that are expressed in my PLV, my entire perception of the situation changed, and my reaction became benevolent and karmic-neutral, if not outright benevolent.

So this was my choice. I could indulge in the moment of anger and try to scare and punish this woman so my ego could feel better. Or I could look at her as a fellow child of God who cut me off for whatever reason she did, but likely did not intend toward me what I was imagining that she intended in my dark thinking. I slowed the car down, giving her reasonable space, and relaxed my body. I started breathing slower and noticing the trees in the fields around me, and what a beautiful place I get to live. I began to entertain alternative thoughts about the woman. Maybe she was ill and rushing to the hospital, I thought. Maybe she has a sick child at home and she's rushing home to save his or her life. Maybe she's distraught over realizing she has cancer and isn't paying attention. Or maybe she is simply unconscious and didn't mean to offend me as I so deliciously imagined, and thereby invited the toxic sanctimony of my anger.

I chose Level 4 in response. It was very rare for me to do so in such a situation. I tend to be more like one of those road rage guys. But the entire experience really moved me for this reason: in a matter of minutes I experienced the power of thought to create our actions that consequently have consequences. Further, our actions create reactions, which, like ripples in a pond, can come back to us as negative experiences created by our original actions. I could've gotten in a car wreck with her, for example. She could've been carrying a gun and felt as if I was the threat and shot me. A policeman could have seen what I was doing by tailgating her and given me a ticket. Any number of things could've happened had I stayed engaged with my anger and my Level 3.

Instead, by calming down through my more benevolent thinking about her, my blood pressure went down and my anger evaporated and my gratitude for the beauty of where I lived returned. As she turned off on a side street, I found myself blessing her in my mind because, in a way, she blessed me. Even though she didn't know it, she gave me a great gift. She gave me the realization that it is not what happens to us in life that determines our quality of life. It is how we react to what happens to us in life that determines our quality of life. And our reactions are based in our thoughts. Our thoughts are guided by our intentions. Our intentions arise out of our identity.

If our identity is a separate ego, personality, history, image, script, and so on, we are going to react toward events that happen to us in life in ways that serve our comfort, security, and image in the world so that we can approach some sense of security, self-satisfaction, and self-acceptance. But if our identity is personified values, our Level 4, we don't take life so personally and we make more objective and better decisions in alignment with the core values and principles that we believe impact all human beings positively.

When we operate in this way, we experience a sense of peace, inner pride, calmness, clarity, and humility. We experience gratitude. And we feel whole, because we feel connected to all other people rather than separated from them.

Perhaps this is what the Bible meant in talking about how we must die to ourselves. Level 3 is a false Self. Level 4 is a true Self. Level 3 is the ego-based identity that most human beings think they are. Level 4 is a Soul-based identity that allows people to move beyond the limitations of their mere personality, history, physical image, experiences, or physical being.

One thing that does occur with great regularity is oscillation from Level 3 to Level 4 Identity, once Level 4 Identity is awakened and begun to be practiced. This often bothers people and has them question their ability to operate at Level 4. That questioning, in itself, is an attempt by our Level 3 to discourage us. Why would it want to discourage us? Because Level 3 is grounded in the ego, and the ego wants to survive.

It is like this: imagine a one-acre plot of land with a white picket fence around it. There is only a small doghouse in the middle of the plot, and patrolling the perimeter of the white picket fence is a large, snarling Rottweiler. He has a spiked collar with a large chain attached to that collar that is secured by the doghouse, and as he walks the inner perimeter of the fence line, snarling and barking at any real or perceived threats outside the fence, the chain drags around with him.

The doghouse that the dog is chained to has a holy person levitating three feet above its roof. Every time the dog goes crazy at something outside the fence that it believes to be a threat, the holy person simply smiles and watches, because he or she understands that the dog is only operating as aggressive and fearful because of its ignorance.

What does that image have to do with this discussion? Everything! The dog is your Level 3 ego-Self, and the holy person is your Level 4 Soul Self. Which one you operate from determines your quality of existence.

As we support people to operate from their Level 4, it is predictable that there will be oscillation and they will be bothered by it. It certainly occurs within me on a constant basis, and Level 4 is pretty much all I talk about all day long with people. Therefore, common sense would say we should expect such oscillation as a natural part of the process.

But how do we recover from our Level 3 once we recognize that we have fallen into that level of identity from our Level 4? You can follow a process that will help you recover more effectively and quickly when you lapse into Level 3 egocentric emotionality. It basically involves a few steps to keep in mind and to practice:

1. First, notice how you are feeling and what is happening around you so you can recognize when your Level 3 is present. Generally, dark emotions indicate a Level 3 Identity.

2. The second step is to consciously remember your three core values and your PLV to filter the situation through.

3. Third, take your Level 4 analysis of the situation and, if appropriate and required, take action from those Level 4 perspectives that are more effective and objective approach to the situation.

4. And the last step is to analyze the difference in how you feel and how the situation has been impacted through your Level 4 actions versus your previous Level 3 actions. Also, how differently you *feel* practicing your Level 4 versus your Level 3 selves. This reinforces your new scripting to more naturally come at situations from Level 4 in the future.

The basic path of recovery from oscillating to Level 3 from your Level 4 involves replacing ego-based emotional decisions with values-based objective decisions. This invariably results in better outcomes over the long term, and typically in the short term as well. Also, the more one practices this rescripting of identity, the more natural and organic you become at Level 4. In other words, oscillation occurs far less frequently with time as long as you devote your awareness to practicing your Level 4 as much as possible.

With time, you will become more and more an organic expression of your Level 4 Identity without having to be conscious of it, and your Level 3 will become more and more foreign to your premise of Self or who you are. As this occurs, life starts to transform in dramatic ways. Some of those ways are these:

- Less stress

- Less fear

- More inner peace

- Better answers to life's questions

- More inspired and better quality of dreams to pursue

- More love and connection to yourself, other people, and life as a whole

- Greater effectiveness in strategic and tactical situations

- More personal power to manifest your future unlimited by your past

- More and deeper relationships with others

- More peak experiences or states of timeless flow

Basically, we suffer distrust in life when we experience a gap, a difference between the nobility of values-based decisions versus the self-serving nature of ego-based decisions. If this happens with ourselves, we know we are doing so out of integrity and we add another rock of evidence to our trunk of evidence against our own character and love-worthiness.

When we declare we are going to improve our health (from our commitment to love of life, others and ourselves), for example, and then we quit working out at the health club after a month, this is experienced as proof that we can't believe ourselves when we make noble commitments because we didn't follow through.

We experience an integrity breakdown that results in self-distrust. And that distrust is interpreted by the ego as a need to get in control still more (to avoid the discomfort of our consequent emotional state), so we double down on still more ego-based behaviors, creating a downward spiral of dissatisfaction.

We are seeking answers in the wrong way and from the wrong source.

So why did we stop practicing our commitment? Because we deferred to our Level 3 in a moment of weakness (for example, it would feel better to just lie in bed this morning rather than go work out; I can do it tomorrow and a host of other excuses). We know we are violating a noble action of stewardship to improve our health out of our Level 4 values through laziness and self-indulgence of our Level 3 choice of this moment's comfort. This often results in even less trust of ourselves when we want to launch new hopes, dreams, and aspirations in the future, so we stop trying.

This may well be a primary component of middle-age crazy and other states of discouragement that we all seem increasingly subject to as we go through life—this distrust of Self and the decisions from that Self. But we make a mistake in this reaction. We are forgetting that it is the source of the decisions we can't trust (ego), not anything more.

And this is the path of mediocrity that Level 3 dooms us to if we don't awaken to the power of Level 4 along with resolved and consistent practice of that higher level of Self, until it becomes second nature, natural, and automatic.

Once that happens, we have finally been born again into our newer, higher Self, and life transforms into a new experience of possibility, rather than being the shopworn experience of just making it through the day.

Finally, considering the likelihood of oscillation between Level 3 and Level 4 identities as we are first beginning to experience and practice our higher identity, it is entirely common to experience self-judgment. But there is a progression path that can be followed to draw encouragement and inspiration to understand where you are and what your next step of progress will be in this growth to Level 4.

COMPETENCY

You may be familiar with the premise of competency as it applies to consciousness. The formula looks something like this:

UI > CI > CC > UC

(Unconscious Incompetence leading to Conscious Incompetence leading to Conscious Competence leading to Unconscious Competence)

The lowest level of competence is when a person is in unconscious incompetence. At this level, an individual doesn't know what they don't know. Imagine, for example, that you and I flew down to the Amazon rain forest and parachuted out of an airplane deep into the jungle. We find a remote tribe. And we approach the chieftain of that tribe and ask him if he knows how to drive a Ferrari. He looks at us with confusion because he doesn't know what a Ferrari is, because he doesn't know what a car is.

To raise his competency level from where he's at, we have to take the next step, which is to introduce him into his conscious incompetence as far as driving a Ferrari. How do we do that? We tell him what a car is, and we show him pictures, and we tell him that a Ferrari is a certain type of car, and we describe how to drive. Let's imagine, further, that we even brought a jeep with us into the jungle, and we put him behind the wheel to have him see that he doesn't really know even how to start it, much less drive it.

This is the second level of competence, which is called conscious incompetence. While it still isn't competence that he is practicing, he at least now has more power in the situation because he realizes and knows that a larger reality exists than he previously was aware of, and that he is incompetent to work within it (that is, he knows what a car is but he doesn't know how to drive a car). This is a higher level of power than to be unaware of incompetence because now, at least, "you know what you didn't know."

So what would we do to raise his power still further? We would put him behind the wheel of the jeep and show him how to start it and drive it with the pedals and the steering wheel, and as we drove around the jungle with him behind the wheel, he would be practicing the next level of empowerment, which is conscious competence. He now knows how to do something, but he has to do it very mechanically, with extreme mindfulness and attention or he will get into an accident.

After the chieftain has practiced driving with conscious competence long enough, he will get to a point where he no longer has to consciously deploy what has now become mechanistically, for most of us, on autopilot to drive a car. This is the highest level of empowerment with anything, true mastery: unconscious competence.

You, for example, may have driven to work this morning twenty-five miles and yet don't really remember the journey. You might play the radio, text on your phone (but we all know you shouldn't), talk to people on the phone. How can you do that?

At the highest level of unconscious competence, where you can do these things like driving a car without having to be so mentally focused, you now have mastered that level of competence where you can do things automatically without having to consciously attend to them with your conscious mind. Unconscious competence is where mastery resides in anything you do in life.

What does all this have to do with oscillation? Especially oscillation between Level 3 and Level 4 Identity? Everything!

The experience of oscillating between Level 4 and Level 3 Identity is actually an experience of oscillation between unconscious competence to unconscious incompetence, and usually only becoming aware of it after the consequences of operating out of unconscious incompetence. You now know that there is this higher level of identity from which you can operate, but now and then you will fall back into your previous script and habit of Level 3 Identity. And when you do, you will eventually notice that you have done so. That noticing is your conscious incompetence.

You may have to practice conscious competence briefly to recover your unconscious competence, but over time, that will be less and less necessary. Simply becoming aware of having oscillated will be enough to take you back to your mastery.

However, in that same process of oscillation, your Level 4 Identity, after being practiced long enough and with enough sincerity to become automatic, allows you to operate in largely unconscious competence with greater and greater frequency and with less and less oscillation.

This process of the evolution of competence and effectiveness is true for most, if not all, evolutionary processes of knowledge and empowerment. But when it comes to Level 3 and Level 4 Identity, it may be the most important place that is critical for you to remain aware of. To remain aware of this tendency of oscillation and the relationship of levels of consciousness and competence as you're going through its evolution is part of the price to be paid to ultimately be able to reside at Level 4 Identity with such consistency that it becomes automatic.

And once it becomes automatic? Your Level 3 Identity is now in the rearview mirror and a distant past that you are no longer subject to. You have now traveled to a place of your own enlightenment that will ultimately help you on your journey home to the destiny and eternity that awaits you, whatever you believe that destiny to be.

At Level 3 Identity you present yourself to the world as your surface features that invite social response. The social response from others is based upon how you look, what you believe in, what your personality is like, and what you have accomplished. That is usually the type of judgment criteria because the social response is based in the motives of a world full of Level 3 consciousness people who want their own egos validated, and their assessment of whether you affirm them and their reality is largely the filter of their judgment, not anything necessarily to do with you at all. This is what defines who you are to the outside world. That world around you reflects back to you with their impressions of you being merely a combination of these surface attributes.

In turn, these reflections invite a likely and strong conditioned response of you trying to either fight their view of you, or prove to them that they should judge differently, out of your own ego-survival instinct at Level 3.

But, at Level 4, this tendency of your identity to be defined by others reflecting back to their impressions of your surface features changes. In fact it does more than change, it transforms. At Level 4, what people now believe about your identity is based upon their experience of you. And when their experience of you is the experience of values (love, compassion, selflessness, humility, generosity, and so on), they reflect that belief back to you by relating to you as the experience of your values. Usually, in turn, they begin to remember (consciously or unconsciously) their own experience of values and often reflect those back to you and those around them.

In effect, Level 4 tends to lift others up to its level of identity more than Level 3 brings others down to its level.

This is the key to your empowerment in life. It begins with you taking on the responsibility of defining values that you believe in being more important than your image in the world. Next, it means you must live those values to the best of your ability as filters of intentions, thoughts, and actions. Next, the world reflects back to you that experience of you being your values, and in doing so, reinforces this higher and more empowered version of yourself. This now becomes the new scripting of the outside world for you: *you are those values*. And when you *are* those values in the experience others have of you, you reinforce that identity within yourself since they have been validated by others.

The world now knows your true identity, and now you do as well: your Soul as it is coming through your values as opposed to the false identity of ego's lesser attributes as a human being with this lifetime.

POP QUIZ

What are some times in your life when you noticed this sort of oscillation of your persona in a situation? When have you noticed, for example, being angry and selfish one minute, but through awareness shifted to a nicer and kinder person quickly thereafter? Put your insights in your journal please.

LEVEL 4: MARRIAGE AND
FAMILY RELATIONSHIPS

Families are the crucible of character
that reveal what ground we have taken,
and what remains for us to learn,
on the Path of Love that is life's ultimate purpose.

"Living at Level 4 has transformed my relationship with family in ways people can only dream about. *To see my children speak from their Level 4 selves is undoubtedly the most rewarding treasure in my life.* **I now know what it means to leave a legacy."**

—*Max Yeater*
CEO/Husband/Father

What is the relationship between Level 4 Identity and marriage and family relationships? Marriage is a formalized commitment of relationship between two people to operate from Level 4 out of love for one another. It is the foundation of modern society, and typically the foundation of family relationships, but not always. It is a crucible wherein the participants are tested constantly as to who they are. Family is an extension of the same principle. Who we are as fathers, mothers, daughters and sons, and siblings reveals who we are at this moment in time as a culmination of everything that has occurred up until this moment in time in our lives, and our scripted responses in return.

As a crucible, a test, a pressure cooker of growth as well as a deep reservoir of fulfillment, marriage and family relationships are some of the purest mirrors we can have for showing us who we are in the world, and to ourselves. This is one of the very things that scares a lot of people away from being married, or having a family. It comes cobbled with tremendous responsibility, not only for the other people involved, but also for growing a better version of ourselves. It is one of the first places that the difference between Level 3 Identity and Level 4 Identity often reveals itself.

If marriage is practiced at Level 4—as personified values committed to bringing those values into the relationship— then the marriage can fulfill its potential to be one of the greatest experiences available to human beings. Being a part of the family that is loving, supportive, kind, unconditional, and nonjudgmental can all be experiences and states that we all want, but often don't experience in life and in relationships.

On the other hand, if marriage or being a member of a family is practice from Level 3 ego-based Self, it will show up as self-serving behaviors: fighting, violence, indifference, abuse, and suffering for all concerned.

It will likely also spell the eventual dissolution of the marriage, if not corrected.

Here is a case study: Imagine for a moment that you are a forty-year-old businessman, homemaker, philanthropist, social worker, farmer, athlete, executive, husband, wife—whichever of these labels or combination of labels applies to you, or even additional labels not on that list. Imagine that you are living a normal life in America today. (This doesn't mean this is only true for people living in America, because it is true for people living in all countries on the planet, but I'm using America for example purposes only.)

Now that you are imagining yourself to be a forty-year-old person on some life path that you are executing in America where you may be employed or not, married or not, happy or not, wealthy or poor, you are likely in the process of living your life every day trying to make decisions out of your Level 3 Identity. For purposes of this process of awakening, imagine a family to demonstrate the process:

Bob is a successful insurance agent at a midsized insurance agency in an average Midwestern city. He makes just enough money to support the family and build his retirement, but is sort of bored with his career and is increasingly wondering whether he made the right choice in pursuing it. He loves his wife and children, but finds himself pursuing outside activities more and more to create a little bit of joy in what feels like an increasingly stagnant existence. His wife, Susie, is a mother of two as well as a successful entrepreneur with her own business as a technical support consultant. They have been married for seventeen years. Their daughter is thirteen and their son is sixteen.

One day, in the course of his work, Bob notices that he is attracted to a coworker. She is younger, prettier, more attentive, and even seemingly more intrigued with him than Susie is after seventeen years. He can't blame Susie, because he certainly has put on weight and is less physically attractive than when they got married, and he knows that he often takes her for granted. He sometimes fantasizes about having an affair with the coworker. He even, with guilt, thinks about her when he and Susie enjoy physical intimacy, which is less and less these days.

Susie feels underappreciated by everyone in her life, especially her children and her husband. She works out regularly and stays healthy, does yoga with girlfriends, and performs her duties as a wife and a businesswoman well despite the busy workload and demands from both domains. She has lately lost interest in being physically intimate with Bob. She feels guilty over that, but also somewhat justified because he doesn't seem to care about his looks as much as she has taken care of her own.

She also fights with her daughter regularly over decisions and feels both close and distant from her son simultaneously. There are times when he is the little boy that she had such a bond with when he was younger, and in other times he is a rude punk who treats her with contempt and indifference despite all that she does for him. For Bob's part, he seems to think that earning the higher income for the family precludes his responsibility in any other area within the family. Susie, accordingly, feels like a martyr in her own household from her resentment of having to do so much more than anyone else seems to do for the family.

Bob and Susie's children are reasonably well adjusted within an average middle-class twenty-first-century American family. However, their children have their own insecurities and have recently begun experimenting with activities that their parents would not approve of. Their parents even sense that something is going on, but they are not quite sure how to find out what it is or how dangerous it may be. Their family seems to have the same situation that so many other families do in their community, where they love each other and yet are living somewhat separate lives within the family context.

They've taken all the family trips that they were supposed to: Yellowstone, Disney World, Grandma's house. While there was a lot of fun on a lot of those trips, they also experienced fights and breakdowns. And the money pressures to continually support the mortgage, car payments, credit card payments, and the latest technology, while paying taxes yet trying to build some net worth for retirement and save for the kids' college seems overwhelming some days to Bob and Susie.

Let's further assume that Bob and Susie's children's names are Jack and Jill. And let's look at what this life is like for them, given that they are all living in Level 3 identities.

Now thirteen, Jill became physically mature at twelve. She is now experiencing the hormones in her body, the growth of a woman's body, and all of the insecurities of middle school. She wants to be liked by boys and liked by girls (for a different reason of course). There is a cool crowd at school, and then there are the rest of the kids. Jill wants to be part of the cool crowd. They often have parties on the weekend, where some drinking, pot smoking, and sexual experimentation is beginning to occur with greater and greater frequency. Recently, somebody said some bad things about her on Facebook, and she cried herself to sleep that night. She likes a boy at school, but he has a reputation for pressuring girls into sexual activity. She has some decisions to make, and she's scared to death of making the wrong ones. She knows that the wrong ones would be in conflict with her parents' expectations as well as her church's.

Jack, age sixteen, is an athlete in his sophomore year of high school, but is only middle-of-the-road relative to talent. For that matter, he is middle-of-the-road as far as his grades, physical handsomeness, and social status. He sometimes has girlfriends, but the relationships only last for a few months at a time and typically end with a great degree of drama. He actually wants to experience sex with his girlfriends, and sometimes they want to as *well, but he always worries about pregnancy, STDs, or getting in trouble with her parents or his.*

He realizes he only has a couple of years before he's going to college, if he goes to college, and is not at all sure that his grades will get him into a school he would want to go to. Or for that matter, why he would even go to college without having any particular passion for a given area of study or profession as an adult. He goes through the normal teenage cycles of happiness to sadness, depression to euphoria, but his euphoric moments are increasingly tied to alcohol or marijuana use. He's basically a good boy, but is uncertain as to who he is or what his future looks like. As a result, he even had some deeply depressing thoughts of suicide if life got too bad. He hadn't told anybody about those, but they scared him when they came. And they seem to be coming a little more often than they used to.

Now, by any standard, Bob, Susie, Jack, and Jill live a blessed life. They have enough food to eat every day of their lives, choosing from the widest selection of food in history. They have a nice house in the suburbs, with a swimming pool in the backyard, high definition television sets, and always the latest computers and smartphones. The kids' college will be paid, one way or another, and Bob and Susie have a standard upper-middle-class American life of relative ease compared to the vast majority of human beings throughout history. And Jack and Jill are the beneficiaries of that circumstance.

So what does this family represent? They represent one slice of a middle-class American family in the twenty-first century dealing with the complex challenges that every generation and family must deal with relative to the paradigm of their time. They also represent that, despite the creature comforts and securitization of life that a successful material existence can create, as it so often does in America and around the world, there is still a depth of suffering present for each of them at times. Is it hopeless? Is it impossible to ever stop the cycles of sadness and insecurity, no matter how materially well-off we are? In my opinion, no, it is not possible if life is lived through Level 3 Identity.

But it is absolutely proven through the experience of countless people that each of these individuals could have a different experience of life if they lived from Level 4 more often. What would that look like?

Let's start with Bob. What might be different for Bob if he approached his life from a more consistent state of Level 4?

Imagine that Bob creates a personalized vision that says this, "My Personal Life Vision is a world where gratitude, integrity, and stewardship are practiced by all and experienced as love."

Imagine that Bob really believes that his PLV is his personal North Star, his personal connection to God guiding him in his decisions in life. As a practicing Catholic, he believes in the church and in the Bible, but lately has been going to Mass a lot less often. His relationship with his religion is more automatic than heartfelt these days, but he doesn't know any other way to try to be connected to God.

He begins to trust his PLV as a more personal, direct guidance system than his religion. He believes that his PLV will bring his religion back to life for him. After all, if he is grateful for knowing that God exists, and his integrity requires him to practice what he says he believes in a heartfelt manner, and his commitment to stewardship requires him to bring his faith back alive, his personalized vision will actually reawaken his relationship with Catholicism.

As we described Bob initially, he is essentially warm, safe, and dry in his daily life, a responsible businessman, and a reasonably good husband and father. But if he died tomorrow, would he really feel as if he had lived the best version of any of those roles?

No, he would not.

Bob knows in his heart that he has to change something within him. So he decides to believe that his Level 4 Identity, as articulated and personified by his PLV, is a higher version of himself. He begins to ask himself questions as to how he needs to look differently at the various domains of his life.

Bob is basically bored with his career, getting bored with his marriage, and is increasingly aware of the responsibility for raising his children without nearly as much joy in relating to them as when they were younger and more compliant. He decides to use his PLV to transform his life.

Bob thinks about his PLV and notices that one value in particular jumps out when he considers his relationship with his career: stewardship. He thinks about stewardship. What does it mean? He defines stewardship as meaning "to design, grow, and nurture effective progress, without personal gain as a primary motive." He realizes that he rarely practices that commitment toward being an insurance agent. So he begins to do so.

When his clients call up, he no longer thinks of them as just a cash register, but instead really listens to their life stories. He gives them the very best advice that he can, even if it doesn't mean any money for him or more business for his agency. He treats them as he would want to be treated. He thinks of them as his own brothers and sisters and mothers and fathers, and therefore gives them the best advice to help them, including referrals to other resources that may help them better than he does. As a result, he starts to feel inspired and fulfilled by his daily work, instead of bored.

Surprisingly, he also notices something else beginning to occur: his business is growing again after years of relative stagnancy. Why? He had always been focused on the money. On his commissions. On what was in it for him, even though he wouldn't acknowledge that consciously. But now his clients are experiencing a new level of authenticity, care, honesty, and genuine concern for what they are concerned about. As a result, they now begin to think of him as a different kind of insurance agent. As a result, Bob's commitment to stewardship actually created the results that he wanted but that were evading him when he was focused on his own benefits. In a way, you could say that his clients were actually beginning to value him beyond the transaction because he began to value them in the same way.

He also noticed that he wasn't as bored by his daily activities any longer, but rather was being inspired by helping other people. Their acknowledgment of his help began to create gratefulness in them that created gratefulness in him for them—as well as a belief in himself that he mattered in their lives and therefore in life itself. He also realized that he was practicing more integrity toward them by treating them as he would want to be treated if he were in their position and was working with someone who truly cared about him and not just getting commissions from them.

He had a great realization as a result of this experience. He realized this great truth: It's not what you do in life that ultimately matters to other people, it's who you are while you are doing it that creates the real value for them.

As a result of what he was beginning to experience in his business, he remembered what he was doing in that business by improving things, and what he was not doing for his wife and children. So he decided to practice his Level 4 Self and to begin embodying his PLV in his marriage and family relationships as well. He began to look at it through his PLV, and the value of gratitude seemed glaringly appropriate. How grateful was he that he had Susie? How much did he take her for granted, assuming that she would always forgive him and be there tomorrow? What would gratitude be thinking and doing relative to his marriage with Susie?

As a result of looking at his wife through new eyes—eyes that were seeing her through the filter of gratitude—he began to treat her with greater kindness. He began to acknowledge all the work that she did around the house, while still trying to grow her entrepreneurial pursuits. Further, he began to help around the house and share the workload without resentment.

He began to sincerely compliment her on how she looked, the things she did, and the qualities of her character that he had grown blind to through the years of marriage and its tendency to numb appreciation. In turn, Susie fell back in love with Bob and began to remember why she was in love with him in the first place. They began having romantic dates and much greater frequency of intimacy again, intimacy that had authentic love as a part of it rather than merely a physical exercise in self-gratification using one another's bodies.

As Bob's Level 4 Identity began to be a more consistent expression in his relationships, he also changed how he was relating to his children. When thinking about them, the value of stewardship became the most apparent one through which to relate to them. He realized that they were growing up. He also realized that they had a right to their own life, and therefore began to look at his control of them through different eyes. Whereas before he was practicing parenting through some tape in his head scripted by books, parents, ministers, and neighbors and friends, now he decided to be a parent through the filter of stewardship and to begin practicing collaborative dialogue about their choices rather than control of those decisions.

Stewardship by parents, after all, must be supporting children in whatever is in their best future interest and their passions, not the parents'.

Stewardship is a very powerful value because it tends to be noble, integrity oriented, and highly objective to achieving the end goal. He thought about his children now as independent human beings whom he loved, and had responsibility toward while they were young, but had a right to their own life path. Accordingly, instead of doing what most parents do with their teenage children and pontificating rules and consequences as a constant dialogue, he decided first to get to know them, in hopes that a more collaborative and teaching role could be awakened rather than the prison-guard-parent style he previously practiced. He felt this would begin with a fresh perspective of whom they actually *were*, rather than his mental model of whom they *should* be despite who they happened to be.

With Jack, his oldest son, he talked with him and found out what he was really interested in. He explored what he could to understand his son's "movie" of life and the world. He began to identify states of angst that he had felt himself at that age, but had conveniently forgotten as he explored his son's world. He realized that some things were the same as when he was young, but many things had changed dramatically. Drugs, alcohol, sex, internet, pornography, ubiquitous programming of fearsome things in life on the nightly news, and seemingly universal victimization were constant themes in his son's world. And on top of all that, his son had just spent ten years in being programmed by a daily diet of apocalyptic projections for the climate that would end the world in his lifetime due to human greed and resource exploitation of the planet.

How did his son even get out of bed in the morning with the heavy weight of toxic programming that had been his experience so far in life? No wonder so many of his friends chose drugs, alcohol, sex, or even suicide rather than face such a world that they were programmed to see.

As a result of his new view of his son, Bob began to treat himself as a steward of his son's future, rather than being a domineering father wanting his son to avoid the mistakes that he had made. He began to take him out into nature—fly-fishing, hiking, skiing, boating, and camping. He began to demand much less of him, but encourage much more from him by talking to his son about his Level 4 as well. His son began to like his dad more. He began to view him as a more complete human being, rather than a prison guard with a wallet. Jack began to smile and relax more around his dad and enjoy their time together in nature. He also began to question following the crowd of his peer group and became more interested in sports, improving his grades to get into a good college, and not going to every party to get drunk until he blacked out.

As Bob looked at his daughter, he also used stewardship as his primary filter for perspective. He followed the same pattern as he had with his son and began having dialogues with her. But the dialogues weren't the lectures that she was used to; they were rather more about her and her world and interests. One night, Jill told him through tearful eyes that her boyfriend had broken up with her. (Bob was so out of touch previously that he didn't even know she had a boyfriend.) Jill shared how her heart was broken when her boyfriend dropped her because she refused to do sexy things with him. It wasn't that she didn't want to, but she was afraid to. Now, her ex-boyfriend was saying mean things about her on Facebook, and recently she had grown depressed. Some of her friends at school cut themselves with razor blades in secret when they got depressed. Bob noticed that Jill had one or two bandages on her wrist while she was saying this.

So Bob didn't react as Jill expected him to. He didn't react as a self-righteous father who was going to punish her for having the emotions and thoughts that she did, or even for some of the actions she had clearly taken that he didn't agree with. Instead, he listened to her, asked her follow-up questions from an authentic and kind place, and when she asked him timidly for his opinion, he gave it through the filter of stewardship and integrity, rather than from his ego, his personality and preferences. Jill began to trust him more. She began to hug him more. Like her brother, she began to do more things with him. They would go bowling, take hikes, fish together, and even go out on father-daughter dates. Because Bob was now seeing a larger side of Jill, and treating her with love and kindness as well as relating to her as her Level 4 Identity (purity, innocence, intelligence), they became dramatically more bonded as father and daughter.

He finally became a Level 4 father for his children and began treating them as Level 4 children at the same time. Now that he and his wife and his children were more authentically bonded through Bob practicing his Level 4 Identity and his PLV in his relationship with them, they each naturally began to do the same toward him and each other. It didn't happen overnight, but it happened over time and with great sustainability. As a result, they finally became an actual family at a Soul level, rather than just four strangers living in the same house related by blood (as is true for so many families that settle for Level 3 relationships).

Bob realized something profound: most parents require Level 4 behaviors from their children (often punishing them when they don't perform as expressions of values), while modeling Level 3 behaviors themselves, which is both hypocritical as well as ineffective. Children learn best experientially, not conceptually (which is secondary and meant to confirm what they are being taught).

Teenagers notice this and rebel against it, to determine that which is true for them on their life path. That causes family conflict.

So by Bob assuming a more Level 4 approach to his teenage children, he actually brought is words and actions into alignment, creating integrity. His children noticed it, and despite their own Level 3 states of evolution, they no longer had his hypocrisy to focus on when violating values and principles that they knew to be right, but violated anyway. Now, when they broke rules, they had to acknowledge their decision to do so and became much more aware of the consequences of those actions—making them better people making better choices. Bob, by taking responsibility for his own level of consciousness, inspired them to do the same, and so they did with increasing frequency.

Bob did two more things as a result of his PLV and his Level 4 Identity; he looked at his health and his spiritual domains of life and realized that they needed work too. With regard to his health, he looked through his PLV and saw the appropriateness of gratitude and stewardship as self-evident filters to improve that state of health. The first question he asked himself was, "What would gratitude be thinking about my health right now?" He did an honest overview of his health and realized that, while he had things he should work on, his overall health was good. He closed his eyes and prayed and thanked God for all of the qualities of health that he was currently enjoying—mental, emotional, physical, and even spiritual.

Next, he scheduled a physical. His doctor told him he had high blood pressure, high cholesterol, and was prediabetic. He recommended a book, *Younger Next Year*, and Bob found it fascinating because it motivated him to begin exercising and taking care of his body. He purchased a rowing machine and began exercising on it every morning before work, building his stamina and strength over time.

He began to monitor his diet much more carefully. More fruits and vegetables, more water, less red meat, in much smaller portions at every meal. His weight began to drop, and his stomach grew smaller, and he had more energy, and he began to look better and feel better about himself, and Susie became more attracted to him physically as a result. He also controlled his high blood pressure and cholesterol and was able to keep diabetes at bay.

Spiritually, Bob was attracted to the word *integrity* as his filter from his PLV. He realized that he had been practicing his Catholic faith through his Level 3 Identity. It had been outside-to-in, in that he had always just followed the directions of the priest. He spent a lot of time committing "sins" that he felt guilty about. He prayed desperately to Jesus in his moments of crisis.

On the other hand, he realized that he largely forgot about Jesus when things were okay. He was treating his Catholic faith as just another duty, another "to do," and as a ticket to heaven rather than as a personal responsibility. "God is not an ATM," he realized. And integrity required that he change his relationship with his Catholic faith. If he was going to commit to being a Catholic, he had to *be* one, not just mimic one through his actions and behaviors. He realized something profound with regard to his relationship with God.

It is not enough to merely believe in Christ, you had to emulate Him.

You had to *be* Christ!

This was a profound realization for Bob. He realized that he had spent his whole life practicing the rules, and rituals, and procedures of Christianity without really taking its essence into his own heart. He realized that he had been operating as the Pharisees, quoting scripture without practicing it. Therefore, he concluded, "Integrity requires that I do my best to live as Christ did in my thoughts, intentions, and actions, not merely proclaim Christ as my personal savior and ignore my responsibilities to do what he said to do."

Bob spoke with his priest about his realizations. His priest was profoundly moved by Bob's breakthrough and privately a little ashamed that he himself didn't even think that way often enough. Bob began volunteering for the church, doing selfless works to help those in need. Ironically, he found that he was going to Mass less often but practicing the message of Mass more consistently. He didn't know what that meant, but he trusted that the authenticity of his intention to be in integrity relative to his relationship with Christ would be how he would approach his spiritual path, whatever the consequences.

As a result, he noticed his inner peace growing along with his sense of faith and trust growing along with it. He began to treat other people, including strangers, with what he thought of as the love of Christ.

So what happened? What happened to Bob in his family as a result of Bob creating a Personal Life Vision and following it to practice his Level 4 Identity as a husband, father, and individual? Bob gained power. Bob gained insight. Bob's family was healthier. Bob became healthier. Bob's relationship with God was healthier. Bob was listening to the outside world less, yet practicing his personal responsibility toward the outside world more. He trusted the values in his PLV more, more than his personality, scripts, excuses, and previous (Level 3) identity habits and preferences.

Bob, through his Personal Life Vision and his Level 4 Identity practice of it, made his commitment to values greater than his commitment to being comfortable. By doing this, he began to live life from the inside-out, far more empowered to impact his future than before. He forgot about the trunk of evidence that he had gathered against himself where he kept his secrets, sins, guilts, and shames. Accordingly, they no longer had power to whisper in his ear and make him choose the lesser path going forward.

Bob was increasingly his Level 4 Identity, although he still periodically oscillated back to his Level 3. But the more he practiced his Level 4 going forward, the better his life got. And the better his life got, the more encouraged he felt, and the easier it was to practice this new way of *being*. His self-confidence grew. His self-acceptance grew. And most importantly, he began to finally love himself. Why?

A person's love of Self is a critical foundation for their ability to be trusted with power in life. To be clear, this is not love of their Level 3 ego, where authentic self-love is actually impossible. Level 3 ego-based Self cannot really be loved because it lives in a conditional reality where love is given and taken based upon an ongoing ledger of performance. All of us, when we operate from Level 3, ultimately remember the contents of the trunk of evidence and therefore fail the test of worth for self-love on a subconscious basis.

A person's love of himself or herself is natural and easy when they are in their Level 4 selves. This is because their identity is no longer their ego image in the world, or their personality, or their accomplishments, but is rather an experience of values for them and other people. It is natural and easy to love the universal positive benefit of values in the people who personify them.

Therefore, while Bob, Susie, Jack, and Jill each have their own lives while being in a family together, who they are within each of those lives determines their self-love, their power, their impact on each other and on other people outside the family, and ultimately their destiny. Susie, Jack, and Jill each had a choice to make like Bob made, and since Bob made the one that he did, it would now be easier for them to choose a similar path. They may or may not choose to do so. That would be up to them. But even if they chose not to follow Bob's example, the family would experience greater love and effectiveness as a family as a result of even Bob doing it.

POP QUIZ

What needs to happen in your family for you to influence it from your Level 4, even if the other people in your family don't respond? Capture your insights in your journal.

LEVEL 4: RELATIONSHIPS

The meeting of two personalities
is like the contact of two chemical substances:
If there is any reaction, both are transformed.
—*Carl Jung*

Living in Level 4 allows my values to guide me, and my intuition to teach me. I consistently experience happiness, inner peace, and fulfillment since becoming aware of Level 3 and 4 identity. My purpose is to bring out the best in others. I have a smile for everyone. We all have equal light within us to share. I am

thankful for my life and the opportunities the universe continually provides. I don't believe in coincidence, rather that every encounter has a purpose.

I am aware of Level 4 Identity because of Al. He is a portal to its truth. In Level 4, we are all one, and the beautiful emotions of compassion, kindness and love fill the most space in our heart and mind. *Our most important task is to seek to reach our potential, being true to our Self and kind to others along the way.*

In Level 4, you learn to let go of the outcome and live in the moment. Suffering is only in the worry of the future or the regret of the past.

Being present and thankful for THIS moment is to live fully.

—Holly Morphew
Entrepreneur/International Speaker/
Business Owner/Financial Expert

Relationships are what create the crucible of societal meaning and interaction in collective activity. Relationships often define us. They fulfill us. They help us experience love and joy and fun and connection and hope. At the end of our lives as we lie on our deathbeds with five minutes left to review how we did, relationships are going to be one of the major vehicles we use to determine how enjoyable and meaningful our life was. Therefore, relationships are where Level 4 identities can dramatically improve the quality of your experience in connecting with other beings.

A person operating at Level 3 consciousness approaches relationships with a user's motivation. It is manipulative at Level 3 because relationships are typically thought to serve the ego-based Self, to help that Self feel happier and better, to be fulfilled through others, and to make "me" look good and feel good about myself. This isn't a bad thing; quite to the contrary, it's necessary as part of our normal development. However, there is a time we must move beyond such self-serving motivations when it comes to relationships.

We must go through Level 3 relationships to understand their limitations and grow beyond them. Level 4 relationships are based on higher motivations than mere self-gratification. Level 4 relationships are based on love, on the awareness of connection and oneness, where we literally merge with other people in a holistic connection and lose ourselves in that moment together. Level 4 relationships are sacred, spiritual, and are explored as different dimensions of ourselves rather than as a separate people in the world whom we must determine to either be friend or foe, as is true with Level 3.

At Level 3, love is often simply a vehicle for attaining self-satisfaction. It is an emotion. It is an action or series of actions. It is a motivation. It's a description of a state of feeling. *At Level 4, however, love is a state of being.* It is ubiquitous both within you as well as the environment around you, because it is a force of nature, an aura that you imbue with whatever is exposed to you. It is just who you are. Just as the sun emanates rays without effort and without separating itself from its rays, the Level 4 person loves naturally and emanates love and therefore is constantly fulfilled by it while simultaneously fulfilling others with it. Level 4 relationships are therefore experiences of unconditional love; whereas Level 3 relationships tend to be experiences of conditional love that constantly fluctuate, and interfaces are far more transactional.

If we use our mythical family as an example, Susie noticed that relationships had grown strange since she'd married and had children. The friends that she once enjoyed now seemed more distant and lost in their own world as she was lost in hers. Oh, sure, she would still go to parties holiday events, and weddings, but somehow didn't feel as engaged or connected to them. It felt more like a ritual and responsibility than a source of regeneration. Susie's relationships had slowly devolved into dusty representations of what they once were. But now she had a chance, through *her* Personal Life Vision, to reinvigorate them and bring them back to life.

Susie had created a PLV in response to seeing the impact that Bob's had had on him and who he was showing up as in everyday life. Susie's PLV said this: "My Personal Life Vision is a community where love, stewardship, and personal growth create a fulfilling sense of family among all beings."

So how did she use this to improve her relationships? Her journey began with her joining Bob as she transformed her most critical relationship commitment: to her family. As she objectively reviewed the "tapes" she was previously playing in her head (as her Level 3 Identity), she found statements like, "I work so hard for my husband and kids, yet they treat me indifferently and without acknowledging me." Also inner statements like, "I feel fat and undesirable, and I wonder if I made a mistake getting married instead of pursuing my career as my only focus." And, "My son is a selfish jerk much of the time, and I am so afraid my daughter is going to get in trouble with sex or drugs or alcohol."

No wonder Susie was quietly miserable and getting more so, right?

So how did her PLV change the internal dialogue (her tapes)? She began with taking the core values in her PLV seriously, as guidance from Divinity (she wasn't as religious as Bob was, but rather saw herself as spiritual and open to a lot of different approaches to connect with the Source). As she thought about

Bob, for instance, the values of love and family became her filter for thinking about him, and she realized that she was expecting and demanding love from him, but not really practicing selfless love *toward* him. She had been creating a ledger of how little he showed his love to her these days and how infrequently they shared physical intimacy.

Now, through her PLV, through her Level 4, she realized that her commitment to the Source required her to *be love*, not just act in alignment with it, much less expect it from others. So she decided to personify love toward Bob, and her children too for that matter, regardless of their response to her. As she began taking responsibility for who she was rather than noticing who he hadn't been, she became consciously kinder toward him, romantic and playful with him, and creative in how she could show him love by helping him enjoy life.

Most importantly, she stopped counting the ways he was showing love to her, yet she felt a dramatically greater experience of love, nonetheless. How was that possible? It was not only possible but inevitable by taking on the responsibility for *being* love, not just expecting love from others. She became an experience of love because she was so naturally consistent in loving without expectation of anything in return. This removes the tendency in other people's egos to process love as merely an emotional transaction. Instead, it awakens in them a place of Level 4 love by experiencing it from someone else—in this case, Susie.

When we experience pure and authentic love from someone else, we somehow automatically move to a deeper place of remembrance. We may remember our mother's unconditional love when we were children in the crib. We may remember a kind minister, a helpful friend, a selfless stranger who acted as a Good Samaritan on our behalf. Whatever our connection to authentic and unconditional love, Level 4 love is not looking for anything in return; it is fulfilled unto itself because of its purity of intentionality.

Bob, in turn, noticed the new Susie and became immediately more drawn to her, attracted to her, and excited by her—and responded in kind. He began to remember what he fell in love with originally when he realized that he loved her enough to want to marry her. He was suddenly blind to her character traits that annoyed him when he was at Level 3. He suddenly realized how critically important she was in his life for that life to be optimized, and he found himself naturally feeling gratitude for their relationship and her role in his life.

Along with her shift toward Bob, Susie also used her PLV to move to her Level 4 in relationships by shifting her internal view, dialogue, and intentionality toward her children and friends. Accordingly, she became an experience for all of her relationships of love, and people began seeking her out to spend time with her. No matter what their response or how much they reciprocated her love, she felt whole, complete, and in a state of love far more consistently. Why?

When a person operates from Level 4 in their intentionality of giving love to others and they become a personification of love, they must create that state of love within themselves to be able to give it to someone else—and by doing so, experience the love they previously only felt they could get from someone else. They fulfill their own Soul's need for love by the benevolence of their intention of becoming love for others. Perhaps this is what Gandhi meant when he said, "You must be the peace that you want for others."

In other words, *we create within ourselves that which we wish for others, and if that is noble and sacred, we create that place within ourselves before we even provide it for others.*

Is this, possibly, what Christ was talking about when he proclaimed that we have "the kingdom of heaven within"? Is this not also what Buddha was teaching? Krishna? The Dalai Lama? Mother Teresa? Gandhi? Saint Francis? All of the high watermarks of humanity?

As we look through the history of mankind, we tend to put certain people on a pedestal. We do this for many reasons: fame, power, impact, inspiration, wisdom, guidance. These figures include spiritual figures, as those noted, and even historical figures. This principle presents itself throughout human history in many forms.

Mahatma Gandhi declared to India that they were going to free themselves from British rule, not through armed resistance and violence, but rather through personifying spiritual principles like truth, love, and nonviolence through passive resistance. He purportedly said, "We will walk them down to the docks and shake their hands and salute them, but they *are* leaving." What did Gandhi personify? Truthfulness, love, nonviolence, courage.

Martin Luther King had a dream that he articulated in his famous speech in which he essentially declared, "I have a dream where, one day, children are judged by the quality of their character, not the color of their skin!" Further, he seemed to almost know his destiny by declaring, "I may not get there with you," which also personified his own faith in the nobility of what he was declaring even though he sensed that he wouldn't live to see it happen.

So Susie discovered that in creating her Personal Life Vision and committing to it, not merely as a set of guiding rules, but as a personal commitment of identity and intentionality, she transformed her relationships dramatically. Her relationships became ever more pure, enjoyable, fulfilling, and inspirational connections to other people—and the Source.

Susie began to look at her children through different eyes as a result of her PLV.

When she looked at Jack, for instance, she realized that she allowed herself to get frustrated by him regularly as a sixteen-year-old boy. He was often dirty, smelly, rude, selfish, self-absorbed, and obstinate. She suspected he was smoking marijuana and knew that he was drinking on the weekends with his friends. His grades were falling, and he seemed to lack all ambition other than to get high with his friends, impress girls, and play in life. "Where is he going to end up operating like he is?" Susie would ask herself.

This way of thinking seemed entirely logical to Susie and helped her feel like a responsible mother from her unchallenged Level 3 Identity. After all, how could observing Jack's irresponsible behavior and worrying about it not be evidence that she was a good mother?

But as Susie thought about her PLV, the value of personal growth jumped out at her. She began to look at her role as a mother through the lens of personal growth, rather than ownership. She realized that Jack did not, ultimately, belong to her and to Bob. While Jack came through her body, she did not own him. His life was his alone to determine, and while she certainly had responsibility to do her part to keep him safe, support his growth, love him, nurture him, heal him when sick, and so on, he belonged to God, the Source, Divinity, eternity—not her.

As Kahlil Gibran famously declared, "Our children are not our children; they are life's longing for itself."

She began seeing where her commitment to personal growth for both herself as well as Jack required her to put a new filter in place in her relationship with him. Her job, she now understood, was to be a force for good in her son's life by supporting his personal growth, rather than to hold him hostage to making her life more comfortable. His purpose in life shouldn't be to make his mom feel self-validated at the expense of pursuing his own life fulfillment. In turn, she also recognized her need to grow within her own life as well, so personal growth became her conscious mantra through which she began experiencing her relationships with both his life and her own.

In other words, by changing the filter of her relationship with her son to one of personal growth, Susie gained objectivity beyond the subconscious parameters that her ego put on her previous premise of *owning* him as a mother. She saw her role now in a more spiritual way. She was to be a force for his personal growth to optimize his future to the best of her ability, and that needed to be the way she needed to talk to him and relate to him regarding his decisions and consequences of those decisions. She would use her support of his personal growth for him to experience her love and stewardship in a new way.

In response to how his mother was now relating to him, Jack started to see his mother through new eyes. Or were they old eyes? Perhaps the old eyes of his soul? Regardless, he increasingly seemed to be reawakening the bond of love that he'd always felt for her as his mother, rather than the more recent feelings he had been growing that resented her because of her constant micro-management of his activities and decisions.

As Susie practiced her commitment to personal growth as her filter toward Jack, he naturally began to soften in his resistance and judgment to his mother's relationship toward him. He began to see her as a human being, complete with all of her pluses and minuses. And he began to forgive her minuses in favor of emphasizing her pluses. That didn't mean that he did everything she wanted him to thereafter, or that he always was nice to her. Rather, it had him begin to at least listen to her, because she no longer seemed to be in constant judgment of him and his decisions.

As they would now have discussions around the breakfast table, she seemed more suggestive and consulting in her approach to listening to his perceptions of his life and what was going on within it. She realized that he was really just a scared little boy trying to act like a man and didn't exactly know what to do next. What he needed, too, she realized, was inspiration and faith in himself. Then he needed to pursue his inspiration and purpose with greater self-discipline. So the question she asked herself was how to get him to be more disciplined—in other words, "How can I be more effective in helping Jack get what he needs, rather than focusing on how right I am and how wrong he is?"

So her discussions with him took a different shape with her Level 4 decision to relate to him as a source of personal growth, rather than as a "prison guard" mom. She began to ask him more questions, rather than always giving him answers. She invited him to explore his options in various situations and quietly pointed out both positive and negative consequences if he were to pursue those various options. She became a "consultant mother" rather than a "management mother." And Jack experienced the difference in a profound way. Accordingly, one day, he approached her very tentatively with something on his mind.

"Can I talk to you about something personal, Mom?" he asked Susie one day.

"Of course," she said with a quiet smile.

"I'm thinking I don't want to go to college when I graduate from high school, but want to go to music school to study music." He asked it carefully, expecting her to explode and tell him he was out of his mind.

Instead, Susie took a breath, thought about her PLV, and said, "Well, honey, that is your decision because it is your life. If you are asking for my opinion, however, I think we should explore why you are entertaining this decision and how committed you are to making it work for you as a career."

Jack was immediately surprised at her lack of anger.

So he relaxed and explored the issue a little greater with his mom. In the end, he felt so comfortable exploring it with her and his father, Level 4 Bob, that they had family discussions about the pluses and minuses of going to college versus going to music school. They only now remembered how naturally talented he was playing seemingly any musical instrument that he picked up easily, and that they sometimes felt disappointed by always having chosen the responsible route when they were his age.

What happened? They explored various colleges and music schools for Jack, and by the following year when he was ready to graduate, he decided to go to college and major in music rather than just go to a purely music school. Accordingly, he changed majors as a junior in college to a double major of both music and accounting, of all things. While he still loved music, he realized that he loved the mathematical precision within accounting and that he happened to be very good with numbers. While his first love and passion was art and music, he liked accounting enough that he had it as a backup if needed if his attempted career as an artist didn't work out—a responsible decision indeed.

Susie's calm, lucid, and objective dialogue with her son allowed him to stay open to her input and gave him the time to explore his various options and, with a few years of growth and maturity, come to a decision that is different from what he thought he wanted at sixteen. That's not only allowed him to come to the decision of how to take a more traditional path in his life regarding his career, but it built the foundation for an adult friendship between himself and his mother.

Susie's Level 4 commitment to personal growth transformed their relationship, once again, into that of a loving mother and loving son. But now that relationship was appropriate to the age of development of each, rather than thinking of him as the little boy he once was. She had unintentionally been holding Jack hostage at that level, out of her attachment to when he was younger, more compliant, sweeter, and more responsive to her.

Susie's relationship with Jill, her thirteen-year-old daughter, was more challenging still. Mothers and daughters often experience a strange sort of sexual competition at a subconscious level. Fathers and sons do the same thing, but between females, it can take a somewhat predictable form. In Susie and Jill's case, the tension had been following a somewhat predictable pattern.

At thirteen, Jill's body had now matured into puberty. Her hormone levels were skyrocketing, and with it the intensity with which she was experiencing all things in life. Boys, girlfriends, changing body, and her annoying parents (especially her mother) were all taking their toll on her psyche.

She had friends who recently began to self-harm by cutting, and while she hadn't done it yet, she had purchased some razors in case she decided to. As a modern young lady, vibrantly in her early teen years, she was deeply engaged in social media. Everything was happening on social media that was exciting, but much of it was toxic (even though Jill didn't recognize it as such).

One day she was texted by her boyfriend who told her he wanted to meet her at the park at midnight. She was to sneak out of her room without her parents knowing. She quickly agreed and begin to get excited over how she would pull it off. She was very smart, so she also realized that the invitation came with the expectation that they were going to engage in sex at a greater level than they had previously. And while that excited her in a certain way, it scared her in another way. But she felt totally alone with the decision and was afraid that he would dump her if she didn't give him what he clearly wanted.

Susie noticed the Jill seemed withdrawn that day. She seemed to have something heavy on her mind. Jill already told

Bob about a party she wanted to go to that night where she would be spending the night with a girlfriend. Susie had her suspicions that that wasn't the entire story.

Susie invited Jill to go to lunch with her, calling it a mother-daughter date. Jill accepted with indifference because she was hungry anyway. They went to a quiet restaurant and found a corner table, and Susie became a different experience for her daughter that ended up changing her daughter's life.

"I invited you to lunch because I wanted to share something very private with you," Susie began. She reached across the table and held both of Jill's hands while quietly looking in her eyes with a sad smile on her face. And she began a confession of a secret that no one had ever known except herself: "When I was about your age, I was in love with a boy. His name was John and I thought that we would be together forever, maybe even get married one day. It felt good when we made out, and kissed, and touched each other. I enjoyed it as much as he did." Her quivering voice quietly explained, "One night, it went too far and we made love. I was afraid and I didn't really want to do it, but things just escalated beyond heavy petting and he was very aggressive."

By now, Jill was laser focused on her mom, realizing this was not a typical discussion. Susie went on, "It hurt like hell, and wasn't at all what I thought it would be and would later turn into with other men that was enjoyable." Susie went on, "The next day, I tried to call him and he wouldn't respond. We broke up the next week. I was heartbroken. Worse, I would find out a few weeks later that I was pregnant."

Jill sat in shocked silence as her mother tearfully continued the story.

"In those days, a girl was thought to be a slut or a whore if she got pregnant as a teenager out of wedlock. I didn't know what to do and was scared to death and deeply depressed, and even thought of ending my life. But, fortunately, my mom, your grandmother, was a woman of great wisdom. So when I secretly went to her and told her that I was in trouble, she simply listened and absorbed the situation without making me feel any worse than I already did."

By now, tears were rolling down Susie's cheeks even though she was quietly smiling. Jill, for her part, was in rapt attention to her mother's story and suspended her guardedness and leeriness of her mother in favor of a new dimension of understanding of all the experiences in life that her mother had already had long before Jill had come along.

Susie continued: "I told my mom that I was pregnant and that I didn't want to talk about how it happened, but that I was thinking of suicide because my life was over. My mom, in a very calm and objective way, simply listened to the whole story and then explored my options with me. One of those options was an abortion. So, without my father or any other family members ever knowing, my mother secretly and quietly arranged for me to have an abortion with a doctor friend that she knew. We never spoke of it again until her deathbed, when I was alone with her and holding her hand as she was passing on. Her last words to me as she lay dying were, 'Honey, you've always been an angel and operated to the best of your ability. Never forget that you are allowed to make mistakes, but you must pay the consequences of those mistakes. You are a warrior of spirit, and I could not be happier with everything that has happened in your life as your mother. I feel honored to have gotten to be your mom!'"

With those words, Susie's mother died.

Jill was silent. She didn't know what to say. And Susie didn't ask her what she thought. They simply finished their lunch, went home, and Susie gave her daughter a hug looking deeply into her eyes. "And, honey, I say to you, from both me and Grandmom, whatever you are dealing with, make your decision through the filter of *stewardship* of your own life, and please be smarter than I was to avoid the pain that I created for myself."

Jill texted her boyfriend that she would not be seeing him tonight after all. She decided to use that as a test of how much he really cared about her, versus just wanting to have sex with her.

Her boyfriend thereafter avoided her and wouldn't talk to her anymore. She accordingly knew that she had just avoided a life-changing decision that could have hurt her tremendously, and silently thanked her mom in her heart.

Jill and Susie never spoke of it again, but Jill's life changed that day because Susie decided to practice stewardship instead of some model of motherhood that she had been scripted into thinking she was supposed to be. Susie's Level 4 awakened Jill's Level 4 and positively and predictably changed Jill's destiny.

With Susie's other relationships, her friends for instance, she began to call them more often and to engage in activities with them. And when she would go to lunch with them, or play tennis with them, or go on a hike together, she found herself more interested in listening to them than talking at them. She began to realize the great truth that everyone is in their own "movie" all of the time, and the rest of us are merely cameo "walk-on" players in the play that they are creating in their minds.

So she listened to them, and when they wanted to know what she thought, she would look at them in their situation through her PLV and let one or more of her values guide her response, rather than letting her previous Level 3 habit of offering opinions based upon self-validating scripts.

Accordingly, and predictably, her friendships begin to grow and deepen. She was suddenly very busy with a lot of activity in a lot of people's lives. They wanted to be around her. She was feeling more fulfilled in her relationships, and she invited that fulfillment through taking on the responsibility of who she was *being* in the relationships from her Level 4 Self. She discovered the great truth that Level 4 Identity reveals: What you intend toward others, you create for yourself.

With Susie's evolution of relationships through her decision to approach them through the lens of her PLV, her Level 4, she noticed that she was beginning to be more grateful for life. She became calmer, more naturally disciplined, and more open to new experiences in life. She was honoring her commitment to personal growth in her PLV by growing into a larger version of herself, a Self that other people in relationship with her increasingly loved to be around because she seemed to bring out the best in them without even trying.

In practicing Level 4, Susie awakened the great blessing of Level 4 relationships that are authentic, deep, truthful, and supportive rather than the Level 3 relationships she had been experiencing as a result of her unconsciously self-serving motivations that drove those Level 3 behaviors.

POP QUIZ

How are your relationships, really? Which ones need repairing and which ones need you to let go of them? Who do you need to be in the relationships you value to optimize them, regardless of if or how others within them respond to you? Note your answers in your journal.

RELATING TO OTHERS AS THEIR LEVEL 4 IDENTITY

Namaste: The acknowledgment of the Divinity, light, or Soul in another person. The honoring of that place in another that also resides in you.

As human beings, a significant portion of our self-identity comes from others. How others see us and what they think about us, whether they believe we are good or bad, right or wrong, share their political or spiritual beliefs—all play into their opinion of us. We constantly go through life subject to the moral codes and scripting of others. Because we are social beings, this is an important and necessary part of human society. However, we can just as easily bring out the best in others if we can help them see themselves as a larger identity. We all have proof of the truth of this if we simply look at a typical dynamic between a good parent and a child.

How do parents relate to their children? Do they hold them hostage for their mistakes in the past? For example, when your child is eight years old and comes to you and tells you that she dreams of being an astronaut, do you dismiss it as crazy because she wasn't potty trained until she was two years old? No, of course not.

As parents (and, I believe, as education from the Source), we naturally treat our children as the futures they are capable of, not the past that they have lived through. This is important to notice because I believe it perfectly demonstrates the possibilities for all of us that we are not stuck with our Level 3 Identity. Nature, evolution, and God have all built into the system the premise that your children are impacted by how you see them. And if you see them as the future they are capable of, rather than the past and their mistakes they've made in the past, how much more likely are those children to turn out as solid, mature, and effective human beings?

And this is the key with other people as well. If you see other people as the future they are capable of and as their Level 4 Identity, even when they are blind to it, you will tend to influence them in that direction into becoming what you see them as already.

When a parent holds a child hostage to their past by constantly referring to their mistakes of the past, they are encouraging the identity of the junkyard dog in the child. However, fortunately, most good parents understand through the power of their love (Level 4) that they choose to see and treat their children as the futures that they are capable of, guided by values that those children need to use for filters of decisions, and they encourage that larger and more optimized identity of that child to come forth.

Perhaps it is this process of naturally treating our children as identities grounded in the futures they are capable of where there is hope for humanity. Perhaps it is through that parent/child dynamic where we evolve humanity to a larger and larger paradigm of consciousness that brings us all closer to our Source, to Divinity, to oneness with all that is—and by doing so, we save the world from our collective Level 3 destroying it.

POP QUIZ

What if, over the next twenty-four hours, you chose to see everyone as having identities as their optimal futures rather than their past habits and mistakes. What would change in how you relate to them, and where might that lead the relationship?

LEVEL 4: HEALTH

Health is, ultimately, balance.

Balance of systems, all systems.

Balance can only arise with wisdom.

Wisdom from understanding,

Understanding earned through the discipline of desire.

Health, therefore, is a report card on your desires.

Al Killeen's "Level 4" awakening has been transformative in all facets of my life. It has provided valuable insight to help me develop "Self-actualization" beyond ego driven tendencies. This tool not only helps develop professional interactions, but also is a fundamental building block to personal/family vision. Al introduced the concept many years ago and has helped me to develop a natural state of being that operates from the perspective of my "Level 4" Self.

The "4th Level" of identity will lay the groundwork of health and prosperity for many generations to come in both my family and any others that have the Courage to adopt this model of self-guidance.

—Joel Horn
Husband/Father/Business Owner-CEO

Health needs to be looked at with a broader eye than we typically look at it. We naturally think of health as merely physical health, but it includes mental, emotional, spiritual, relational, career, and other types of health too. Balance is the key to optimal health within those various domains, as well as for your overall health.

Actually, one of the first clues to our level of identity and consciousness is how we look at health and respond to it. From Level 3, we typically think of health as primarily physical health. We then become aware of mental and emotional health when we are in trauma, but rarely look at relational health, spiritual health, or even occupational health.

While Level 3 looks at health through a narrow lens of primarily physical health, Level 4 naturally has a much broader view. At Level 4, health is thought of more holistically rather than as the often superficial and mechanical perspective that Level 3 tends to have. Health at Level 4 means a holistically balanced and effective and functional system, in all ways. These ways include physical health (of course), mental health, emotional health, spiritual health, relational health, family health, occupational health, and many others.

I can use my own example of operating at both Level 3 and Level 4 when it comes to my health.

When I turned sixty, I went in for my annual physical. Dr. F. is a wonderful doctor and very reasonable, without any apparent ego and always inclusive to his patients' perspectives. He commented on how I was already on statin drugs for high cholesterol, blood pressure medicine for high blood pressure, and was now thirty pounds overweight and prediabetic. (Remember Bob's story? My own experience is where that story of his health came from.)

When he shared all of this with me, which wasn't new information but rather a reiteration of what I already knew, he asked me, "I've noticed that you're on all these medications for these conditions, and it seems to be getting a little worse every year, so what's going on?"

I'm ashamed to admit to you that my response was flippant, but honest at that moment from my Level 3: "Frankly, Dr. F., I don't give a shit!"

He laughed and said, "Will you at least read a book for me?" I promised I would, not expecting in the least that I would do whatever the book said to do because I had read seemingly every book on health and exercise and had failed so many times before in trying to be motivated by all those books to get healthier. I had secretly resigned myself to whatever happened to my health just being my destiny.

On his recommendation, I promptly bought *Younger Next Year* by Chris Crowley and Henry Lodge and began to read it. That book was so impactful that after only reading two chapters, I went out that weekend and bought a $5,000 elliptical machine and began working out on it every morning for the next five years. My cholesterol dropped to normal, as did my blood pressure. I lost the thirty pounds I was overweight, and I literally reversed the aging process from the trajectory that it was on. I recommend that book to this day, and everyone I recommended it to has had the same experience I did and changed their path of physical health going forward.

So what does this have to do with Level 3 and Level 4 Identity? My Level 3 Identity had lapsed into a lazy pattern of self-indulgence when it came to diet and exercise. My Personal Life Vision, my Level 4, was awakened by that book to have me begin to care about myself in a new way and have faith that I could have far more impact on my health in the future. That inspiration and faith caused me to change my pattern of behavior relative to working out and literally change my body's chemistry.

In the end, I began to care about myself in a new way because of my commitment to the values in my PLV (realizing my fullest potential, for example). This is just one example among countless examples I could give as to how my Personal Life Vision has made me a better human being, with greater empowerment, greater effectiveness, and a greater commitment to even wanting to be alive and do something great with my life.

And that is all waiting for you as well.

Write down your current level of health on a scale of 1 to 100 for each domain of your life: physical, mental, emotional, spiritual, relationships, career or occupation. What would you like to raise the numbers to? How can you invite the values in your PLV to design a pathway to execute to get there? Write down your answers.

LEVEL 4: OCCUPATION

If fear drives you, you will pursue activities
that will seem to make you safe.
If love drives you, you will pursue activities
that awaken your soul.
If you believe that an awakened soul
is the most safe place you can be,
you will guide your ship by the North Star of love
and practice your occupation as an
expression of that guidance.

Giving away my power to fuel others in their times of powerlessness is my one true path to peace. Al's concepts, including that of living a life of Level 4 existence, resonate with and have encouraged me on my path of lawyering with strength and compassion. May you find what you are missing in the pages of this book. Thank you, Al, for your influence, friendship and water cooler conversation.

—Patricia Bellac
Lawyer/Advocate/Servant/
Adventurer/Wife/Mother

What is your occupation? You may notice that I didn't ask what your job was. That's because your occupation may or may not involve working at a job. It may be being a mother and a homemaker (which, of course, is the toughest job in the world, but more importantly an occupation grounded in service and love).

Your occupation is how you spend the majority of your time in your life that creates something your life needs. For most people, that is money. For other people, that may be something other than money such as love, legacy, or contribution.

What is the relationship between your occupation, what you do every day, and your Level 4? Your level of identity that you design and practice your occupation with will determine not only your effectiveness within that occupation, but whether that is even the proper occupation for you in the first place.

In other words, your occupation is an opportunity to create or produce something for the world that can help the world as well as your life proceed forth and evolve to help with survival, building net worth, building relationships, or any number of other motivations and outcomes.

Your occupation is often how you spend the majority of your time. It is also often the legacy that we leave behind. So let me ask—are you pursuing an occupation that best reflects the highest part of you, a place or an activity where you can practice your core values on a constant basis? If it is not, you may be "leaning your ladder against the wrong wall." You may be going down a tunnel that is a dead end. Or you may do perfectly well at creating revenue to fund your life, but at the expense of your fulfillment and sense of significance and joy in life.

And shouldn't an optimized occupation be one that fulfills these life needs along with economic needs?

So how do you use Level 4 to impact what you do all day every day—your occupation? It might be easiest to describe a contrast with what occupations pursued from Level 3 often look like compared to occupations practiced from Level 4.

Let's look at Bob and Susie again to process how your level of identity and consciousness can impact occupations.

Bob, remember, is a classic family man. He is a successful insurance agent at a midsized agency. He has practiced this line of work for decades. He makes an adequate living, enough to support his family if they are not too extravagant. How did he get into this line of work? He became an insurance agent because he was recruited out of college and was desperate for a job. He didn't particularly love it, but now that he had momentum within the profession and had done it for so long and had developed so many clients, he sort of felt as if he could never leave it without having to start over. In a sense, he felt he was held hostage by his occupation as an insurance agent.

As Bob became more comfortable and habituated in using his PLV as his filter as to how to "see" things, he reconsidered his tendency to build a case against his occupation as an insurance agent. He began to treat his clients through his core values of stewardship and integrity, which were both front and center to his PLV. When he handled client calls, he now tended to enter into his business conversations as more of a listener and really tried to discern the objective reality of the client's situation, as well as their perception within those objective factors. Instead of his previous Level 3 tendency to resent calls for claims, he saw that, through stewardship, these were people in need to whom he and his insurance firm had made promises that he needed to fulfill. He realized that his clients were really no different than he, and that they simply needed help from him, which he was now increasingly grateful and happy to provide.

Accordingly, Bob's relationship with his daily activity as an insurance agent moved from being daily grist for the mill of seemingly pointless activity to earn money into a new North Star for him, an opportunity to practice stewardship on behalf of others.

Accordingly, Bob began to look forward to going to work because of his different mind-set and heart-set that he had created out of this new attitude toward his occupation. He no longer saw it as simply exchanging time and energy for money, but rather sought as a crucible of contribution through which he could impact the lives of others and reduce their suffering. That aligned for him in a deep and profound way, and he was able to begin to connect his attitude at work with actually practicing his spiritual beliefs, rather than merely mimicking the rituals on Sunday mornings.

He began, for example, to more consciously practice the Golden Rule of treating his clients as he would like to be treated.

His reward was a newfound passion for an old activity of occupation, one that grew his inspiration for life and his self-acceptance as a person who was making a difference in the lives of others, which allowed gratitude and fulfillment to be more ever present for him at work.

Susie, on the other hand, who is a homemaker as well as an entrepreneur with her own online business, also tended to practice her daily occupation with a greater sense of a to-do list than actual inspiration for doing it.

In her role as a mother and homemaker, she sometimes felt guilty over her resentment of her husband and her children. They didn't seem to appreciate what she did for them (and appreciation for people practicing this type of occupation is typically all the direct compensation they get). In her better moments, Susie forgot her resentment (martyrdom?) in favor of the love that she felt for her husband and children, and in those moments, she enjoyed and was grateful for the role rather than resentful of it.

After she had created her PLV, Susie began to take a far more proactive role in her relationship with her various occupations. As a homemaker, she began to see that her PLV could be and needed to be at the core of her "why" in doing her duties.

She recalled a quote she had read in college by Nietzsche that said: "He who has a *why* to live can bear almost any *how*."

She realized the truth of that incredible quote by understanding that she now had that "why." It was her Personal Life Vision.

As she thought about her Personal Life Vision, she certainly valued the stewardship that she was practicing in her role as a mother and a wife, but the two values that really jumped out at her were love and personal growth. She saw that, from her Level 4 PLV identity, her children and husband were people that she loved. She realized her responsibility to not merely practice the activities that implied love, but that she literally had to *be* love for them in their experience of her. For that to happen, she needed to stay mindful of her "why" as she was doing her activities for them and do them with a joyful heart and a loving intentionality.

By doing this, she knew that they would be more likely to reciprocate and be as she was being. This would fulfill the covenant of love that is implicit in every marriage and every family, but is too often lacking because of the Level 3 hijacking of personal egocentric motivation.

By practicing her PLV in her role as a homemaker, she now set the standards for which the rest of her family could learn to practice love in their lives through the dynamic of the family bond.

When it came to her business as an entrepreneur, she also saw that she was very blessed to be able to pursue an activity that she was passionate about because she didn't have to focus on how much money she made. Bob made enough money to support the family with his job as an insurance agent. Susie, therefore, had an easier time of connecting her PLV to the "why" of her business choice as an entrepreneur because she wasn't blinded by the requirement of returned compensation as an eclipsing motivation.

As she executed the duties of her business, like Bob, she began to treat her clients as more than just vehicles for compensation. She began to see them as individual human beings with the full panoply of challenges and blessings that all people experience in one way or another. She decided that her value proposition was actually the way she made her clients feel through their experience of the values in her PLV, not her activities or what she was selling.

Those activities and what she was selling were merely the canvas upon which she was painting the masterpiece of connection, faith, love, and trust with her clients. As a result, she also began to enjoy her job in a new way. It was now more than just a way to survive; it became an atmosphere of awakening for her learning and inspiration for life itself. And since love and personal growth within her PLV leaped out at her as the appropriate values through which she could create an "art" of her occupation, she looked at it with new eyes.

She decided to start each day with love in her heart for herself and everyone she spoke with that day. As a result, her clients sensed the difference and began to see her in new, engaged, and connected ways. She deployed personal growth by starting to require measures of growth and improvement of her effectiveness as a business with new levels of accountability. That, in turn, had her create written project plans for growth of business, which soon resulted in significantly greater sales. And even though that wasn't her motivation (that is, to make a lot of money), her personal growth of accountability and effectiveness had that result nonetheless.

She began saving the extra income for a beach home for the family one day in the future. The home that love built for her family through her business.

Bob, in his daily work at the insurance agency, had become familiar with a similar oscillation of resentment for the bureaucracy and corporate nonsense that he had had to put up with on many days, contrasted with the joy he got when he helped a client with a problem that they were having in his role as an insurance agent.

In other words, both Bob and Susie had experienced the shift from their Level 3 to their Level 4 identities in their occupations, but often didn't identify them as different levels of identity. Instead, they simply experienced the fluctuation of satisfaction and fulfillment with their occupations on a relatively daily basis without having any real control over when those states of mind visited them.

However, once Bob and Susie had created their PLVs, and through those PLVs had begun to consciously practice their Level 4 identities in relationship to their respective occupations, the paradigm of their relationship with work literally transformed.

Work was now a vehicle for them to practice their PLV and the values within those PLVs in their daily activities. This completely shifted their relationship with how they spent their days. Instead of some burden to bear in the name of economic compensation, they now saw that the money they earned was simply a symptom of a greater process they were engaged in. They were now vehicles of hope, support, love, and connection for all the people that they interfaced with in their daily activities. It became a win-win relationship with the people around them. The clients and teammates at work now received better treatment and better service than they were paying for, and both Bob and Susie felt a deeper sense of significance and passion for their daily activities that seemed now like they mattered far more than how they appeared to on the surface of the Level 3 world.

Another thing Bob noticed was that his son was now starting to wonder about what he wanted to do for a living. He was only sixteen, but the society around him constantly warned him that he would fall behind, starve, and live a life of very few choices if he didn't make a lot of money. At least that is what his parents had constantly harped on as long as he could remember: the fights over money and how it was spent.

Ironically, as much as Bob had disliked his profession much of the time, his Level 3 Identity as a father often had him encouraging Jack to follow precisely the same pattern and script that Bob followed. However, within Bob, when he looked at his PLV and what it required him to focus on in the way of the values that it declared, he began to look at Jack differently.

The values of gratitude, integrity, and stewardship are all at the heart of Bob's PLV. What jumped out at him when he thought about Jack's future were the two values of stewardship and integrity. By asking himself how he could best support the son he loved through those values, he realized that his commitment to stewardship required him to do what's best for Jack, not what relieved Bob's fears about Jack's future.

Stewardship, in other words, required a values-based and objective approach to solve the problem of what Jack's occupation would be. Integrity required that Bob be honest about his own dissatisfaction with the path that he had pursued. Integrity also required Bob to notice the value of a passionate relationship with his occupation, rather than a fear-based relationship that merely allows an occupation to create financial resources for survival. Stewardship as a value further helped Bob recognize that Jack making a good enough living to support himself wasn't necessarily a competing commitment with him pursuing his passions, even if those passions were in areas of life that Bob didn't know anything about (in Jack's case, it was music).

Accordingly, Bob began to listen more closely to Jack when Jack was sharing his dreams about the future. He noticed that Jack often spoke about careers in music, art, and even going off to a third-world country to help the citizens build houses or improve their health. Although Jack had made a responsible decision to have accounting as a second major in college—in case music didn't work out—he still was impassioned about trying a more exciting and purpose-driven career first.

Bob recognized the idealistic, yet noble intentionality of young Jack's dreams. And listening to those dreams, Bob experienced the debate in his mind between his Level 3 fears and his Level 4 commitment to Jack out of integrity as a steward of love for Jack's optimal future. So Bob found himself helping Jack research options toward his passions, rather than just seeing how he could get him to take a job as an accountant just so he could support himself.

As the years rolled by, Jack ended up going into artistic pursuits and philanthropic pursuits in the initial phase of his career. He never made much money, but Bob noticed he seemed grounded, mature, happy, inspired, and purpose driven. He never did become an accountant, but years later, after becoming a quietly successful music producer, he did find that his accounting background helped him understand how to manage his personal and business finances. Life is like that. It gives us tools today that we will need tomorrow, even if we don't recognize it at the time they are given.

Bob, almost guiltily, began to feel somewhat jealous of how much Jack loved doing what he was doing as he pursued various activities in the direction of his dreams, rather than just selling out to his fears as Bob had done with his occupation. But, then, Bob would realize that such jealousy was, in itself, a

Level 3 response from his ego trying to feel better about itself. Upon this realization, he simply replaced such thoughts with his PLV and, upon doing so, awakened to the realization that he loved Jack and therefore wanted only good things for him—and music seemed to be a good path for him.

In other words, Bob's Level 4 reminded him that Jack's life was his own, and Bob's role within it was to be a steward to help Jack optimize that life, wherever it took him, because that was what love would do. Love wouldn't make Jack's choices based upon Bob's validity as a father. Love would allow Jack to have his own walk with destiny.

POP QUIZ

Are you in the right occupation? Are you working at the right company? Are you in the right culture? Answer these questions through your PLV (that is, can you practice your values in your current occupation, even if you aren't particularly inspired or comfortable in your role?). Note: The "right" or "wrong" occupation is not a matter, necessarily, of how comfortable you are (Level 3 motivation), but rather how committed you can be within that occupation to express your higher Level 4 Self. Write down your answers.

LEVEL 4: BUSINESS

Work is love made visible.

—Kahlil Gibran

I almost missed meeting Al Killeen in the summer of 2014 as I was teetering on not attending a meeting where he was presenting. As Al presented that morning, I knew within a few moments that a spiritual influence had stepped into my subconscious on why I was not to miss the Integrative Mastery Programs presentation that day. The daily journey from here to eternity that began with Al's presentation has continued to be enhanced over the past 3 years.

Through the Level 4 experience I learned from Al; my relationships are enriched with my wife, family and others I meet in the walk of life. The awareness and practice of Level 4 Identity beyond the daily grind of an ego-based existence helps bring recognition, awareness and mindfulness to my relationships with everyone; that life can be simple, peaceful and purposeful when present in the moments of every day.

So profoundly did I see the power of a Level 4 existence and training, I introduced Integrative Mastery Programs to my business partners so they, too, could have the opportunity to enrich their lives. Further, now our company incorporates this Level 4 cultural values program into our company training.

—Paul Duncan
Husband/Father/CEO

Shifting to business, what would Level 4 generate in a business environment as a contrast to Level 3? If we think about the nature of business today, we observe a fairly definable and predictable pattern. Organizations are founded, funded, grown, and managed for the purpose of some return on investment. In the case of for-profit organizations, that return on investment is typically money. For nonprofit organizations, that return on investment is enough money to administer the organization's personnel and resource compensation requirements for basic operation and growth, but also compensation in the form of satisfaction that good work is being done to help other people.

Accordingly, business is an institution that has great possibility when it comes to the application of Level 4 consciousness in the world.

To appreciate the significance of the impact of Level 4 Identity for the world, we must take a broad view of business and its place in society. In the twenty-first century, humanity is at the pinnacle of its evolution thus far for human beings. Think about that. You, dear reader, are living at a time of the pinnacle of human consciousness and societal evolution in all of history. What is the optimal perspective you might want to have in order to take advantage of that gift, contribute to that evolution, and impact the world to come?

If we take a brief view of the flow of history, at least using Western civilization as an example, we can see a clear pattern of evolution occurring in the realm of consciousness. Imagine the following stages of evolution over the last few thousand years as being in four phases:

PHASE 1: THE CLASSIC PERIOD

From approximately 500 BC to 500 AD, Western civilization was dominated primarily by ancient Greece and Rome. This was a time where the interface between individual human beings and society changed form. The ancient Greeks founded most of the current structures of modern civilization, added to, and evolved further by the Roman civilization.

While Judaism had been created prior to this period as one of the primary religious traditions of the West, during the Classic Period, Christianity, the second of the three dominant major religions of the West, was established. This was also the period when modern artist expressions were refined, democratic principles were established, and the promise of individual worth and freedom within society was being redefined. Technology was advanced in significant ways (for example, the utilization of cement in ancient Rome allowing aqueducts to be built that stand to this day, because a material was finally discovered that could be molded by man, yet stayed strong as a rock in water).

This era in history was ended by the intrusion of the Germanic tribes of Europe, the Vikings, and other groups who helped bring down Rome from being the most powerful empire in the world. After Rome fell, the next phase began.

PHASE 2: THE MIDDLE AGES OR DARK AGE PERIOD

During this time, society was governed by monarchies in the secular world, and the Catholic Church in the religious world. Islam, the third of the major Western religions, was founded in this era, and while it had its period of spreading into the West, Islam was ultimately forced back into the Middle East for further growth into the current era.

Meanwhile, in Europe, monarchies and Catholicism (the dominant sect of early Christianity) reigned supreme for the majority of this period. In European society, the people generally had a monarch at the top of society (along with other nobles and wealthy elite that comprised 1 percent of the population), with 99 percent of the rest of the people being peasants who were there to serve the monarchy and the small upper class of feudalistic landowners.

The Catholic Church generally held domination over the religious trajectory of society in the West, with Protestantism only arising late in this era. This overall period lasted from approximately 500 to 1600 AD. During this period of time, few people had a high quality of life. Most were starving peasants, living hand to mouth with disease and privation commonplace. This was a prescientific era when superstition and plague ruled Europe. People were now concentrating in larger and larger population centers, but without scientific understanding of pathogens and basic sanitary requirements of compressed populations, disease and crime were rampant.

Many scholars refer to this as the Dark Age because it represented a perceived devolution of society from the organized and unified world that Roman and Greek domination represented. This ultimately led to the next evolutionary phase, the Newtonian Scientific Period.

PHASE 3: THE NEWTONIAN SCIENTIFIC PERIOD

From approximately 1600 AD to the middle of the twentieth century, Western civilization suddenly experienced a burst of knowledge and forward progress in the arts, science, and technology. Newtonian science began to see rational scientific methodology as a means of figuring out tangible reality with greater predictability, and mankind now saw the power of analytic thinking become predominant in the primary guidance structures of health, science, and social structure.

Western civilization now had the rise of government, with many different experiments as to how government should organize society, but with an eye on individual opportunity and freedom also being desired by the common man and woman. This was when the rise of democratic institutions and new ways of looking at how society and civilization interfaced with individuals and their freedom and rights. In the eighteenth and nineteenth centuries, we had the burst of representative government structures present themselves as alternatives to the old system of monarchy. Now, instead of monarchies, we had new experiments with systems defining how government would interface with individual human freedom, rights, and empowerment. This was when America was formed. This is when the American, French, and Russian revolutions all took place that overthrew monarchies.

This rise of rationalism and scientific methodology created tremendous benefit to raising the standard of living for all people, yet had its limitations as well. For one thing, due to the obvious benefit that hyper-analytic objectivity in the form of scientific methodology gave humans for advancing beyond widespread emotions and fears (by creating predictability in the future rather than superstition-based beliefs), rational and tangible reality became the only reality that could be trusted. This gave great power to the collective Level 3 of humanity since rationality became the primary tool that society used as its North Star. And since objectivity and tangible predictability are primary vehicles that the ego uses to express power and control, rationality now became "God" to a scientific community that was now explaining reality to the rest of us beyond the mysticism and superstition that religion seemed to represent.

Since religions and spirituality lacked the tangible proof of veracity that scientific methodology is based on, they became quaint individual beliefs that a person may or may not adhere to—but certainly not above the obvious higher truth of tangible objectivity. People continued to believe in a spiritual context and necessity in life, but hard-core scientists know how to objectively cite a more provable, and therefore more truthful, mental model of reality.

The Catholic Church saw Protestantism be born, as well as the challenge for the religious domination of people to now be shared with many other faiths and religions. As humans expanded aggressively over the globe, technology allowed the overthrow and outright elimination of native ethnic groups all over the non-Western world in a rush by Western powers to control natural resources as foundations for empire building and technological and military dominance—all as expressions of progress. This destruction of ethnic spiritual traditions was primarily driven by the collusion of insistent religious Christian dogmatism and aggressive power growth by Western European powers to legitimize their so-called superiority.

During the twentieth century, the two primary forms of interface between governments and individuals in the West became a battle between authoritarian collectivist idealisms, such as communism and socialism, confronting and battling with representative capitalist and free-market democracies. One believed in the power of government over the individual in the name of equality and fairness. The opposing belief system emphasized the power of the individual and in the human soul to be a creative force for good, as long as it was unleashed from excessive governmental constraints.

During this period of time, certain societal institutions were tremendously empowered: family, church, media, nation-states. But following this period, beginning in the early twentieth century, the rise of new ways of looking at the relationship between individuals and civilization, as well as the relationship between the dominant secular and spiritual traditions, shifted one more time to the newest paradigm of reality in Western civilization: the Quantum era.

PHASE 4: THE QUANTUM INFORMATION PERIOD

The name of this latest evolutionary phase comes from the discovery of quantum mechanics in the early to mid-twentieth century, which evolved Newtonian scientific understanding beyond the limitations of tangibility-based hyper-rationalism. In studying the micro world of atoms and subatomic particles, quantum physicists found a world where the rational rules of Newtonian science no longer applied. Why did this matter? I believe this because the quantum world is the bridge of a larger understanding of ultimate reality between the tangible predictability of scientific methodology and the intangible world of energy, consciousness, and spirituality.

In other words, our current era is where science has a chance to synthesize into spiritual understanding, creating an entirely new paradigm of reality for human beings—and you and I are on the cusp of that.

Stephen Hawking, for example, once made a remarkable statement. "*If we discover a complete theory, it should in time be understandable by everyone, not just by a few scientists. Then we shall all, philosophers, scientists and just ordinary people, be able to take part in the discussion of the question of why it is that we and the universe exist. If we find the answer to that, it would be the ultimate triumph of human reason—for then we should know the mind of God.*"

Some examples that I've heard about in the wondrously mystical world of quantum physics and how it changes our understanding of reality include some of the following examples.

When observers in a laboratory observe photons, which are subatomic electromagnetic elements (including light), they impact the way the photons appear to them. If they expect photons to appear as particles, they do. If, on the other hand, observers expect them to show up as waves, they do that.

In other words, the smallest observable particles of matter (quanta) that form the foundation of all of the larger forms of matter, of which you and I and the apparent world around us are a part of, are impacted by our consciousness and its expectations of how to see them. This is sometimes referred to as the observer effect.

Some other examples I have heard of include the ability of particles in one location showing up at a distant location before they've ever left the original location in the quantum world. There are also stories of how subatomic particles separated at a great distance resonate with one another and begin to mimic the rotation and direction that the distant particles are moving, even when there is no known connection between them through the ether.

Last, in studying the microscopic world of atoms and subatomic particles, scientists have discovered that these amazing little foundations of everything that we observe are, in fact, merely energy fields of probability rather than solid matter. In other words, our reality is based on subatomic particles that have no real mass. They are simply energy fields of probability awaiting influence from some other force to take observable form that we can experience at our level of gross perception.

What does this mean? It means that our consciousness is the only known influencer that we know of in the universe that impacts the way material reality formulates—at least that we participate in with daily experience that can be predicted. And what is consciousness?

Nobody really knows. Neurological and systemic expressions of it can be measured and somewhat defined, but consciousness itself is a primary mystery to modern science, even to this day. Therefore, it may be whatever we believe it to be, and I choose to believe that it is that part of us that we share with the Source, with God. And the more advanced we practice that consciousness is a measure of how empowered we are within its influences, since it is a part of that force that created and manages the entire system of reality we call the Universe.

Level 4 is the next level of that empowerment principle of consciousness, in my opinion and experience. To participate in the greater influence Level 4 can give us, it requires that we leave behind what we otherwise believe our Selves to be—Level 3 Ego-Self. Experts in quantum physics are probably groaning as they read what I just wrote. But one of the amazing things about quantum physics is those who have studied it most say that it is impossible to fully understand with the human mind, because it moves beyond the parameters of rationality, which we require as the framework of understanding and truth.

I've come to believe that everything in reality simply "is." In and of itself, it has no meaning. Everything that we spend our time judging and labeling and assessing and evaluating does not have the intrinsic meaning we give it, until we give it that meaning with our minds.

In other words, our entire reality is colored by our consciousness, whether we know it or not. While, at first, this may seem to deny the role of a greater universal power that has predefined the meaning of all things, but what if that power gives us the opportunity to turn reality into what we expect based on our level of consciousness?

Isn't that what may be indicated by the observer effect of quantum mechanics?

Is this literally true? Well, the question I ask myself is whether or not the universe would continue to proceed as it does even if humans were not in it to observe it. My conclusion is, I don't know. Does our consciousness create the environment for the universe to exist as we see it? Or does it exist independent of our consciousness? Perhaps it's the age-old question of whether or not a tree falling in the forest would still make a sound if there were no humans there to hear it.

Either way, it is clear that our consciousness is the most wondrous aspect of our existence, and we have a choice of either guiding it or not with our intentionality. A Personal Life Vision is the vehicle to do just that. Only it influences reality toward the light (through values), rather than the darkness (through our self-serving ego), and creates reality for us, accordingly.

So an individual operating at Level 4 out of a chosen identity of Level 4 is an embodiment of the values they are emulating, and Level 4 therefore becomes a critical vehicle for manifesting the version of reality that allows us to experience life in the light, rather than the dark.

In the current and newest paradigm of human evolution in Western civilization, many of the institutions that were present in the last expression of societal evolution are under assault and in decline. Governments are being challenged by individuals more than ever. Nations' borders are being dissolved in the name of open and free societies for everyone. People are leaving churches in droves. Families are, sadly, declining and morphing into new structures for individual commitments. Divorce is now more common than staying married in America, for instance.

But there is one institution on the rise worldwide that now has increasing power and is a finger pointing to the future: the institution of business. Business, as an institution, is on the rise everywhere in the world. Even the Chinese communists are becoming entrepreneurs in the business realm.

Along with the evolution of society, government/individual interface, technology, and information systems has come the growth of knowledge, and that knowledge is available as an amplifier of human consciousness. You can go to the internet, for example, and find out how to heal a sick child as easily as how to build a terrorist bomb. Your decision to do one or the other will be made by your consciousness.

Therefore, consciousness is the most powerful variable controlling the future of humanity, and Level 4 consciousness is accordingly critical for humanity to be evolved benevolently into a better reality for all. The alternative is a set of Level 3 societies that could be worse than the Dark Ages, since we now have the technology to destroy the entire world if our power is not managed properly.

Accordingly, there has never been a time when Level 4 Identity is not more critical. Now that we have the internet, and the free flow of information at a level that has never occurred before, we have an acceleration in the power of individual humanity. That power can be used for good or for evil, depending upon the consciousness level of the individuals utilizing it.

There's never been a time in history, for example, where virtually any individual with access to the internet (which is now ubiquitous throughout the world) can find out how to make a nuclear bomb that can cause world-changing devastation. At the same time, the internet and the free flow of information has provided access to virtually all known human knowledge through Google. People are now far more capable of making choices toward the positive, if they choose to do so.

Level 4 Identity is, in essence, the decision to be a force for good in the world. This is opposed to Level 3 Identity, which is a choice to practice self-serving behavior, which can periodically advance the world (through competition, for example), but often is self-serving, selfish, and negative for humanity as a whole.

Business and the intentionality and execution of its goals are therefore a major institutional force toward either the good of humanity or damage to humanity. What determines how any individual business ends up *being* is based upon the value proposition of the business, the culture providing that business value proposition, and the consciousness level of the leadership of that culture within the business. Level 3 leaders and managers leading organizations tend to create cultures that often provide lots of problems through the interface of various Level 3 egos within those business cultures, which is experienced by the customer as indifference, bureaucracy, and a lack of true authenticity of care.

However, business that is led by Level 4 leaders create cultures that tend to reflect the consciousness of those leaders and become Level 4 themselves. These Level 4 organizations and cultures actually operate as expressions of the values they say that they stand for in their corporate vision statements scrawled boldly across their walls, as opposed to those simply being dead words on the wall. This is in contrast to the all-too-common experience for the employees and for the client experience if they are culturally practiced as mere ideals expressed by Level 3 leaders who don't actually practice or acculturate them into the organization.

Simply put, business can be viewed as the hope of the secular world as long as it is guided from Level 4 consciousness.

Last, consciousness is the greatest influencer of actions and outcomes in the world, and it has evolved faster and faster over the history of mankind. For example, the relative consciousness of an average person living in 3000 BC wasn't all that different from someone living in 1000 AD, for example. Yet how different is the general consciousness level for people living in America today from someone in 1000 AD?

It is clear that consciousness is expanding three dimensionally in all directions at an ever-increasing speed. If you saw it as a chart, you could go back 10,000 years and see the graph of human consciousness barely rise from 8000 BC to 1500 AD, but subsequent to that period has increased the angle of evolution steadily upward until it has curved up into a seemingly vertical direction and speed of evolution over just the last forty years.

This book, for example, was written in 2017 in digital formats and printed in a digital and electronic format. I was sixty-five years old. When I was born in 1952, the reality was more like this:

- Thirteen-inch black-and-white TVs were so rare that neighbors would stand outside the houses of people who had them and watch through the windows. (These were not color, by the way, and certainly not 65-inch HD quality, with only three channels if you were lucky to have all three networks, and programming signed off the air at midnight.)

- No fax machines, no personal computers, no internet, no cell phones.

- No iPads, iPods, no DVD players, no iTunes.

- Cars weren't all that dependable, and there weren't fast-food restaurants on every corner.

But technology and information empowerment has accelerated to such a point that you have more processing power today in your cellular telephone than the astronauts had to make it to the moon. People all over the planet now seem to own smartphones that give them access to this technology, even in many third-world countries.

How does a person keep up, much less thrive, in such a fast-paced and evolving world?

By being grounded in your PLV values and knowing that you are doing all you can to make the most of your life as you want it to be—for yourself as well as for others out of the nobility and unconditionality of your values.

POP QUIZ

How consistently are you remembering that your activity in business is not just about the money, power, or prestige, but rather about the fulfillment you can experience by practicing it from your higher rather than lower Self? Write down your answers.

LEVEL 4: ACCOUNTABILITY AND EFFECTIVENESS IN LIFE AND BUSINESS

Integrity is the correlation of your words and actions.
Accountability is the purest expression of that relationship.
If you demonstrate accountability,
you demonstrate integrity;
if you lack accountability, you reveal that you lack integrity,
and integrity is the critical foundation
of trust and effectiveness.

Using these principals has transformed my life. *I have witnessed a remarkable, even enviable culture emerge in my organization.* **By operating from an Undifferentiated, Empowered, Values-Based Self, it has given others around me the safe space to bring their best selves forward. There is considerably less stress and anxiety in my life as well.**

Thank you, Al, for bringing this awareness into my life.

—*Phil Shell*
Husband/Father/Real Estate Executive Manager

Your relationship changes dramatically at Level 4 with both accountability and overall effectiveness in all domains of life where you apply it. The reason this happens is fundamental. It is best understood by contrasting Level 4 with Level 3 approaches to accountability and effectiveness.

At Level 3, ego-based identity, we have a tendency to be scripted into external accountability relationships. Parents, teachers, policemen, and Walt Disney all guide us as to what we should do if we want the consequence of being perceived as good.

Obviously, the opposite is true as well. We are warned against poor behavior and poor accountability with negative and uncomfortable consequences. We tend to be scripted into a reliance upon external resources of accountability (bosses, spouses, friends, coaches, social forces, for example), which impacts our effectiveness. After all, if we are dependent upon external accountability resources for being our most effective Self, what does that imply we are when those resources are absent?

Our effectiveness is also compromised at Level 3 because we have the ever-present concern of perception of others and how we are either adding to or taking away from our trunk of evidence that we hold against ourselves as egos.

At Level 4, all of this changes. If we are identified as a personification of love, for instance, our love for ourselves as well as all other beings will require us to operate with intrinsic accountability when we make promises and commitments. We will also be more objective in what promises and commitments we make, therefore precluding overloading our schedules unnecessarily. This overloading can occur when we seek to please others as one of our primary priorities in life, which is built into an ego-based identity.

But at Level 4 our accountability becomes internal instead of external. We hold ourselves accountable to what we say we will do out of our commitment to the integrity of our values. Further, our effectiveness dramatically increases in regard to our relationships, jobs, tasks, and projects because we now operate in the realm of objectivity and analysis of situations, no longer hobbled by the subjectivity that is intrinsic to an ego trying to avoid putting more evidence in the trunk against itself.

In other words, despite the belief within the ego to the contrary, Level 3 is a disempowered, passive, and indirect relationship with accountability and reality as a whole; whereas Level 4 is an empowered, active, and direct relationship with accountability grounded in self-guidance through the PLV.

Better results are accordingly experienced with accountability through Level 4, as well as all other aspects of our life experience, because we have the benefit of an active and responsible foundation.

POP QUIZ

Are you being accountable to your responsibilities from an internal commitment or merely via external consequences? Write down your answers.

LEVEL 4: INTENTIONS

How people treat you is their karma;

How you react is yours.

—*Wayne Dyer*

Learning and being aware of the need to live at "level-4" resonates in my heart. It requires that I view people thorough a prism of compassion. That I live daily in gratitude and react to obstacles with determination to do what is right, not what is best for me or what feeds my ego. *It encourages me to work towards realizing my goal in life; that of becoming more Holy in a very broken and unholy world.* I owe a debt of gratitude to my friend and mentor Al for this enlightenment.

—*Ben Zitting*
Husband/Father/Top 1% Mortgage Lender

Intentions are at the heart of differentiating Level 4 Identity from Level 3 Identity. When a person operates from Level 3 Identity, which appears to be the vast majority of people, 98 percent of the time, their intentionality is intrinsically focused on their self-interest. I personally believe this is because of our drive to survive.

If you are familiar with Maslow's hierarchy of needs, one of the lowest levels is that of survival. Beings have an innate drive to survive. In human beings, this is thought to be located in the limbic/primitive brain system. This is the oldest part of our overall brain system. The purpose of the primitive and limbic brain complex is to run the autonomic nervous systems of our body along with creating the survival instinct, and the emotional/ego responses to survival threats.

This phenomenon is explored beautifully in a book called *A General Theory of Love* (by three physicians, Thomas Lewis, Fari Amini, and Richard Lannon), where the various "brains" we have are detailed in their writing. Alligators, for example, only have a primitive brain (which, in humans, is subordinate to our limbic/mammalian brain). That primitive brain is incapable of bonding, emotion, and love, which becomes the job of our limbic emotional brain to respond to. Accordingly, 90 percent of baby alligators are eaten by adult alligators out of the two things that drive all alligators operating from their primitive brain: the autonomic nervous system (to keep their bodies operating without having to think about it) and survival.

When we operate as our egos, we operate out of a place very close to that of alligators: eat the other guy before he eats you!

When we operate out of the unchallenged identity of our Level 3 ego, we are operating out of old scripts that we created as a result of our experiences in life. Those scripts include our programming by the institutions of authority around us: our parents, siblings, ministers, teachers, cops, cartoons, and even Walt Disney. On top of that, our experiences within the family unit often determine our trust or lack of it in life itself. It can be harder, for instance, for the child of a mother addicted to crack (who is indifferent and abandoning) to trust the world once that child grows up. Even for children who grow up in loving and attentive households with great parents, if what they experience on a constant basis is the articulation of noble values and ideals but the experience of selfish behavior, the message of living by values doesn't really sink in.

Too often in this world, children are taught that they should be one way (values guided), even though their parents don't model that behavior. That doesn't make their parents bad people. It makes them human. Their overall brain has the noble idealism of values in mind, values that they might learn at church or from some other institution. But they don't always practice those values in their actual interface with other human beings when operating out of their Level 3 or limbic brain—including model behaviors around their own children.

Level 4, however, has an altogether different intentionality as part of its architecture. Level 4 is, by definition, an *identity* and therefore an intentionality to actually *be* the values that are otherwise merely noble ideals in the Level 3 world. Using the Christian belief of the Divinity of Christ as an example of the highest among us, it brings to mind the story of the adulteress in the New Testament. The way the story goes, at least to my limited knowledge, is that the Pharisees brought an adulteress before Christ. They declared that she had violated "The Book" (which was, essentially, the Old Testament). She had committed adultery, and The Book said that she must be stoned.

"What do you have to say, Rabbi?" they demanded of Christ. "She violated the rules in The Book and it says she must be stoned."

How did Christ respond in this moment where his destiny could be determined by how he replied? If he denied what the Pharisees were saying was in The Book, he would be accused of blasphemy and crucified. If he confirmed what they were declaring as being in The Book, then he would have to agree with stoning her to death, and he would fall back under the subjugation of their model of how The Book must be honored at all costs.

He would also violate something even more important: his Level 4 personification of compassion, love, and nonjudgment.

This is offered as an example, not as any sort of endorsement or critique of one religion over another, but as a classic example of the difference between Level 3 and Level 4 consciousness. What did Christ do in this moment where he seemed to be trapped by the strategic brilliance of the Pharisees' question?

He changed the conversation profoundly.

Instead of responding with the two choices that the Pharisees presented, Christ responded in an altogether surprising way.

"Absolutely!" he declared. "That is what The Book says. So the first among you *without sin* cast the first stone."

This revelation stopped the crowd from stoning the woman to death. Instead, as the people in the crowd looked into their own hearts, they realized that they were sinners as well and dropped their stones, saving his life as well as that of the adulteress. The Pharisees were shamed into seeing how they were so focused on the letter of the law of their religion that they were violating the foundational spiritual principle of nonjudgment and compassionate love.

What was Christ doing in this interface? He was operating as an example of a Level 4 intentionality of love and nonjudgment interfacing with the sanctimony and self-righteousness of the Level 3 Pharisees. I believe this particular story represents a perfect interface of what we go through every day in our own lives as individuals.

We are constantly faced with the choice of listening to the rules in our mind that are part of our script, but ignoring our heart, intuition, and deep inner knowing of what is right. In other words, our head often overrides our conscience, our heart, our spirit. But the opportunity of Level 4 is to invite intentionality that is in flow with universal values that I believe are the language of Divinity within humanity.

When we operate from Level 4, our heart is in charge of our intention with our brains in the service of the heart. The heart begins to guide us (which one could say is guidance from the Soul, and therefore our connecting point to Divinity, God, or the Source), and our head is the functional apparatus for executing what the heart decides. Values awaken the heart and operate from a larger truth than our individual ego-based mind-scripts are capable of.

Accordingly, identity creates intentionality, and intentionality creates thoughts, and thoughts create actions, and actions create consequences and results. If we begin at the root of that process—our identity—we influence everything that happens after that beginning point. Level 3 intentionality is accordingly destructive much of the time (because it is rooted in self-interest). Self-interest is innate to human beings as part of the survival instinct. Therefore, since we cannot change that, all we have the power to change is the identity that the self-interest is serving.

Level 4 Identity has a Self that is no longer limited to just the individual's personal being. At Level 4, the Self includes all humanity, not merely the individual within which it is occurring. This makes Level 4 Identity a trustworthy and benevolently intended and perhaps even divinely guided force for good in interfacing with other people. Therefore, since intentions are what end up creating the manifestation of desired outcomes, and intentions are grounded in identity, the larger and higher and more noble the identity, the greater the results.

This sounds idealistic, fantastical, or unrealistic, but in essence, it is simply taking responsibility from a higher place within you to guide your mind by larger and universally experienced values rather than from the scripted and habituated (and much more common) route of external expectations responded to as various levels of personal comfort. Since this interface with others' approval of us and our resultant comfort is largely grounded in the past, in what we are familiar with that makes us feel safe, Level 3 guides the individual to simply reaffirm their past habits of response (in the form of past conditioned responses to the expectations of others) into the future and, therefore, is a barrier to greater knowledge, growth, and fulfillment.

Therefore, Level 4 Identity is the path to personal empowerment, meaning, and an optimized life through the innate nobility of the intentionality contained within it being guided by values rather than being limited by egocentrism—and the resulting karma that comes from that egocentrism. Think about it, how much suffering do you personally know of that was rooted in decisions, actions, and interfaces with Level 3-based behaviors? Drunk drivers killing people, people physically abusing other people, countries attacking other countries?

I believe that the majority of human suffering in life, at least in relation to relationships with other humans, can only be ultimately resolved by the evolution of human consciousness to Level 4. This doesn't mean that everyone has to get there, quite the contrary. If even a fraction of humanity evolves to Level 4, the "ripples in a pond" impact of those individuals can tip the scales of the future of humanity toward the light, toward the good, and toward an ever-increasing level of understanding as to the sacred gift of life itself.

Wayne Dyer wrote a wonderful book some years ago called *The Power of Intention*. This book was very insightful as to how intention impacts our daily reality through sculpting our perspective and revealing what our deeper desires can be. Further, the book points out how we have influence over our intentions in a very real way, and by practicing that influence with a responsible attitude toward our highest Self, we can experience profound transformation in our physical, mental, emotional, and spiritual realities.

This is a fundamental point to optimizing your life. Where does intention come from? There are many answers to that question, but I prefer to look at it through the following pattern of power within us:

- Our consciousness invites a choice of identity.

- Our identity, once chosen, determines our intention.

- Our thoughts are created from our intentions.

- Those thoughts create perspectives, choices, and actions.

- Those perspectives, choices, and actions create subsequent actions.

- Our actions influence and impact our experiences in reality.

- Our experiences of reality either cause our ego reaction based in comfort (Level 3), or our values reaction based in commitment (Level 4).

And that reality responds to those influences and impacts in either comfortable ways or uncomfortable ways.

This is a model that not only works in a linear and unilateral direction from consciousness to results/reaction, but it also is influenced the other direction upstream. In other words, our results/reactions in our life can actually work all the way upstream to impact our consciousness, *if we apply mindfulness.*

What is mindfulness? Mindfulness is our chosen awareness to be present, objective, and as complete as possible as to the entire reality around us at any given moment, on all dimensional levels.

Since consciousness can only be sculpted by our influence over time using mindfulness, which arises after a series of collective experiences that have us choose to be in a state of present-mindedness or not, we have to initiate all activities beginning with the original direction and flow of these events.

So the first point that we have any real power to impact our results, which can create this cycle in one direction that then circles back to its beginning and can create an upward spiral and evolution of our power, fulfillment, and optimize results, is starting with identity.

This is precisely why the four levels of identity are so critically important to understand and to consciously practice. The real opportunity in all of this is to practice awareness of Level 4 Identity in a Level 3 world.

If you think of animals and the way that we believe they currently operate, they lack self-awareness as a separate ego, by and large. In other words, dogs can't get conceited. We can anthropomorphize their personalities to proclaim them as such, but they actually are unaware of what they are doing (but perhaps most egocentrics are).

When human beings operate at their Level 3, they are essentially just operating at a more sophisticated expression of their animalistic level of consciousness. What is Level 3 Identity for both animals and human beings? It is using the script of experiences of the past along with other people's perspective on who we are that has us assume that we are merely a collection of those events. The stimulus of other people's perspectives on us, as well as the experiences themselves, are then immediately measured relative to their "comfort quotient" for us, along with whether they potentially represent discomfort or a threat. Then, our Level 3 reacts accordingly.

And those reactions create karma, either good or bad. There is a reason why it said in the Bible, "What ye shall sow, ye shall reap."

In other words, as human beings grow up and go through life experiences, including the opinions of others and their scripting of that individual (scripting from parents, teachers, friends, mentors), their consequential karmic reactions will be experienced. But Level 4 Identity is possible only through the free will of conscious choice that we have as human beings. And to unlock the door of the power of Level 4 Identity requires us to use that option of free choice to override our scripting and past experiences in favor of a newer, larger identity that associates values as our higher commitment and Self than mere validation of conclusions drawn from the past.

Level 3 protects what we already know and allows us to temporarily feel comfort as knowers. Level 4 invites more to know and therefore invites growth from being learners. Learners grow, knowers stagnate.

When we choose our Level 4 Identity of personified values overriding our habituated identity of our past scripts as Level 3 ego-based identities, we now open a door to a new reality that invites power, fulfillment, and enlightened understanding of why we are even here in the first place. When we do this, we no longer operate at the level of the animal, but now we operate at the level of the angel, Divinity, and Christ consciousness or God consciousness or Buddha nature. Level 4 Identity is, therefore, achievable only through *awakening* our larger identity of Level 4.

So how does intention interface with this dynamic? When we choose our Level 4 Identity of personified core values, our intention is prepackaged out of the values that we have chosen, along with the nobility of having made the choice to personify those values. We have the right to define those values in our own way, of course, but we find that the values themselves have a consistently benevolent meaning to most people, and therefore minor differences in definition don't end up mattering in the end.

After we have consciously chosen our Level 4 Identity, it then naturally follows that we deploy intentions in alignment with the values of our new identity. Those intentions then create thoughts that create actions and perspectives that end up fundamentally transforming the outcome of events. So while choosing Level 4 Identity is the first critical step, intentionality is where we can begin to see the first expression of that new identity through the clarity and nobility of our new Level 4 intentions toward the world in contrast with our ego-based, and often petty and toxic, intentions toward the world that can come from a Level 3 Identity.

To repeat, the Bible said, in other words, you reap what you sow. In Hinduism, Buddhism, and many other spiritual traditions, the concept of karma is present. Karma occurs as a result of our actions, either good or bad, pleasant or unpleasant. If we desire to have pleasant, fulfilling, and ever increasingly joyful experiences and results in our life, it naturally follows that we have to create intentions, thoughts, and actions that will lead to that space. That process is created from our Level 4 Identity.

By contrast, our Level 3 Identity is grounded in an ego-based assumption of Self, and therefore often creates the karma that leads to the majority of suffering in our lives. And on the subject of suffering, it involves more than what happens to us. It also includes how we perceive what happens to us. And this is another place where Level 4 Identity saves us. If we stay in our Level 4 Identity of seeing the world through personified values, our interpretation and perception of events is now colored by those filters.

Accordingly, when something occurs that invites our perception of discomfort, unfairness, or pain, our conclusion about those events changes when we choose to perceive them through our filters of Level 4 Identity as somehow associated with a reflection of certain values. We don't react out of Level 3, and therefore avoid making the situation worse and amplifying its potentially dark karma.

For example, I was having a conversation with my son the other day about the dangers of alcohol as a habit. I tried to set the conversation up very carefully to keep his ego asleep so I could talk to his higher Self. I made logical points as to the dangers of alcohol currently existing on an epidemic level in society and how those dangers seem to be largely ignored until it's too late and too many families suffer as a result. How alcoholism creates tragedy after tragedy on a global basis that is ignored, because the judgment of the Level 3 Identity world doesn't want to lock itself out from its ability to indulge in alcohol either.

My son was in his Level 3 Identity for a portion of the conversation, so his ego interpreted what I was saying as a personal attack on his decisions. At other times, he would hear me through his heart of love, his Level 4 Identity, and he would be calm and able to have a dialogue about the issue from an objective place. Level 3 Identity is grounded in ego and ego personalizes reality to constantly assess whether it is hurting or helping. That ego becomes a powerful block to objectivity and creates thoughts and actions that lead to dark and toxic decisions and actions, which often result in toxic outcomes that create negative karma and suffering.

POP QUIZ

How consistently do you monitor not only your conversations or actions, but the intentions behind those activities. Where are three areas in your life where you may be able to dramatically alter outcomes by improving the quality of your intentions? Write down your answers.

LEVEL 4: THE PRAGMATIC UTILIZATION OF MYSTICISM IN EVERYDAY LIFE

Al has been a great support to me in attaining and maintaining my "Level 4" (as he calls it) consciousness. At the risk of sounding a bit "woo woo", *the greatest impact that operating in concert with my calling (at Level 4) has is that when I make my mind up to accomplish something, the world seems to bring the people, events and even the resources needed to fulfill on my commitment.* **As the 18th Century German Author Goethe said: "the moment one definitely commits oneself then Providence moves too. All sorts of things occur to help one that would never otherwise have occurred."**

—Brad Zimmerman
Husband/Father/Business Owner/Trainer/Coach

Our Level 3 Identity is intrinsically suspicious and doubtful when it comes to the value of the intangible—experiences difficult to measure and difficult to experience with our normal five senses. This is logical. Our analytical mind is what helps us determine the patterns of the world and whether those patterns can help us or hurt us from a survival instinct. And since our ego is rooted in the survival instinct, and all of the subtle variations therein (judgment from others, for example), we automatically are suspicious of the intangible and the mystical when we operate from Level 3 Identity.

After all, how can an ego protect its worth if it is dealing with something intangible that can't be measured? Additionally, self-preservation of the ego-Self automatically seeks control of the environment it is in, to prevent risk to body, image, position, and power. The illusion of control is very important to a self-concerned ego-Self, and the experiences of life that are intangible don't allow such control. Thus, the intangible, experiences that require faith, areas of life where the image of the ego can't be presented in a fashion likely to create a response of approval must be suspect.

However, try on this perspective. Imagine that placing your highest trust in the ultimate intangible—God/Source/enlightenment—is what Christ, Buddha, Gandhi, the Dalai Lama, and all the other holy ones have actually given us as the *most* pragmatic template for how to live life we could imagine, but we have largely missed it, due to our Level 3 Identity self-protection tendencies.

When a person operates from their Level 4 Identity, not only filtering their reality through their values but actually personifying those values as their primary filter for interfacing with life, a certain kind of magic happens. For example, when Christ told us to love one another as we would love him, what happens there?

If we literally practice what Christ and the other holy ones have told us to practice in our interface with life, we must create the love within ourselves to love one another truly before it ever leaves us. Accordingly, the very thing that our Level 3 seeks through the eventual response from external circumstances and people (love, in this case), is automatically present within us the moment we intend toward others. That, in turn, naturally has us full of love before we even begin to interface with others, and it also creates the karmic response to love as opposed to some lesser intention that is felt by the other parties when we operate from Level 3. Thus, given that everything tangible ultimately arises from the intangible, even according to quantum physics, Level 4 Identity provides a pathway to making a process of pragmatic effectiveness in life very natural and real in a consistently experiential way.

This is the subtle universal truth underlying all spiritual traditions that seems to have largely been missed due to the conscription of the great messages that have been given to us by the holy ones. These universal messages of truth were often subsequently processed through a to-do list to negotiate positive consequences.

In other words, at Level 3, we tend to follow the teachings of the holy ones in hopes of getting something by doing so. Perhaps if we are acting as they have told us to act, for example, we will get into heaven. But Level 4 understands that it is the front-end intentionality grounded in identity that determines whether we create consequences that are (hellish), or we create (the kingdom of heaven within) before we even begin to interface with others, much less their response to us.

POP QUIZ

How frequently do you allow yourself relief from the unchallenged tendency to quantify, measure, and/or judge everything and everyone around you, and even yourself? How often do you allow yourself the delicious freedom of peaceful acceptance of the unknown, the mystical, and perhaps even see the quietly divine hand of God working magically through the unexplained, the "coincidence," the mysterious and magical? Write down your answers.

LEVEL 4: FLOW

When I let go of what I am, I become what I might be.

—Lao Tzu

While sustaining Level 4 is an unrealistic expectation for any earthly being, knowing

it exists and working to continually strive for Level 4 allows us to occasionally experience it for both short periods and sometimes extended durations of enhanced consciousness, fulfillment, and peace in knowing all is as it should be. This is sometimes referred to as being in "flow" and that is exactly where and when amazing things happen in our lives, families, and businesses. Brother Al I want to thank you for helping me to identify my Level 4 through a personal life vision and coaching me over the last few years to more frequently experience the "flow" as I am definitely enjoying the ride!

—*Eric Amhaus*
Husband/Father/Business Owner-Partner

You may have heard about the term *flow*. It is a term that is increasingly being used to describe people who are operating at an optimized level, often seemingly without any effort to do so. Some examples might include Michael Jordan playing a game of basketball in the championship finale where there are two seconds left and he, smilingly and calmly, takes the inbound basketball, dribbles twice, jumps from an absurd distance, and easily swishes the winning basket for the championship—all with a smile on his face and his tongue hanging out (his trademark body language when focused in a basketball game).

It is the ballerina in the middle of a perfect performance, the ice skater who is creating superhuman feats of strength, and the master musician playing a song that awakens your spirit.

And flow is in you, and me, and everyone else who has ever lived when we are in a state beyond the limitations of our inner dialogue assessing our performance and judging it. *Flow is when we enter into a state of masterful performance without the need for the guidance system of commentary from our brains.*

There are components to achieving flow. A person must have the capacity to practice their craft, whatever it is, at a masterful level. Malcolm Gladwell in his book *Outliers* says that it takes 10,000 hours to achieve mastery of anything. Perhaps that is true, perhaps not, but most human beings have experienced moments when they perform an action in an almost perfect way and do so with such ease that it almost seems as if it wasn't them even doing the action.

According to the leading psychologists, the state of flow has certain definable attributes: Time stops; cognitive thinking skills are seemingly natural and without effort; inner peace, a certain knowing of what to do without having to think about it, a sense of almost witnessing your own performance as though from the outside takes over; and masterful execution of the required actions without hesitation happens.

These are just a few of the attributes people describe when they are in a state of flow. So what does Level 4 have to do with the state of flow?

Everything!

One way that a person recognizes they are in a Level 4 Identity is whether or not they are in a state of flow. When a person is in flow, they are naturally and calmly guided by their heart in their direction and intentionality, but facilitated by their brain as to how to execute the steps necessary to achieve what they are envisioning from their heart.

It is the state of pursuing passion and inspiration with resolve that is often beyond our commitment to being comfortable, yet we move forward nonetheless. Why? Because in moments of flow, we are more committed to realizing what we are envisioning in our minds, but we see the task from our heart more than we are concerned with being comfortable. When we are in this state, our future is no longer limited by our past. That is because the past is what evidence we have gathered as to the rules that we set in our brains for how we must guide our future actions, almost like a prison guard guarding a prisoner.

And that is why our typical state of activity when we are not in flow is representative of our Level 3 Identity. It is the ego monitoring the illusion of Self—being merely my separate Self in my individuality.

By contrast, when we are in Level 4 Identity, we live in the moment (another attribute of being in the state of flow; being in the now). When we are at Level 4, we naturally live in the moment and focus with complete and seemingly effortless concentration on whatever we are doing without being burdened by a constant inner dialogue measuring our effectiveness along the way. This allows all sorts of mechanisms within us to come into collaborative play together to create effectiveness. This can include intuition, body mechanics, muscle memory, and a billion billion neurons operating in concert to create a symphony of effectiveness of our activity aligned with our intentionality.

If this is typically a reflection of us at Level 4 Identity (that is, being in the state of flow), why does this state of flow occur when we are in that level of identity?

Because when we are in Level 4 Identity, which is, remember, undifferentiated, empowered, values-based Self, we have a larger sense of Self that doesn't require us to limit our mind to the parameters of linear analytics. Rationalized reality, or linear analytics, tend to be home base for Level 3 ego-based identity. This relationship with reality is rooted, in all likelihood, in the need to control to survive, as previously discussed. Level 4, by contrast, allows us to experience effective actions without the effort that our mind constantly requires of us as our Level 3 requires us to deploy through corrective measures and judgments of our analytic thinking.

So the relationship between Level 4 Identity and flow is one of several levels intertwined. When we are in Level 4 Identity, we tend to experience flow very consistently and naturally. When we are in a state of flow, we naturally tend to invite our Level 4 Identity because we lack the need for the constant self-judgment that comes from the rational/analytic totalitarianism that occurs out of Level 3 Identity and its need to manage behaviors from a punitive premise.

POP QUIZ

What are some areas of your life where you experience flow? When was the last time you did something at a masterful level without having to even really try? When were you last in flow, and how did you feel while there? What might increase those experiences in your future? Write down your answers.

LEVEL 4: CONSCIOUSNESS, SPIRITUALITY, AND RELIGION

I believe in God, but not as one thing, not as an old man in the sky.

I believe that what people call God is something in all of us.

I believe that what Jesus and Mohammed and Buddha and all the rest said was right.

It's just that the translations have gone wrong.

—John Lennon

While I continue to learn and practice every day how to "be" my best "Level 4" Self, the experience of truly focusing on it has changed my life for the better in so many ways, but particularly in my relationships with other people which are much more positive and rewarding than before.

My Level 4 Self has allowed me to be a more understanding Christian; a more loving husband to my bride of 44 years; a more inspirational father and grandfather; and a more insightful and patient leader, coach, and manager in my chosen profession of Mortgage banking.

Thank you Al, for helping me be a Better ME!

—*Gene Humphries*
Husband/Father/Grandfather/
Division President/Believer

Consciousness is the whole and complete awareness of our *being*. It is often thought to be largely synonymous with spirituality. Spirituality is the environmental state of spiritual energy within and around us—the intangible source from which we came, and the etheric and benevolent intelligence that has designed and is guiding the upward process of evolution within that awareness to which we are connected and inseparable from eternally. It is a different dimension we can access at any time, a dimension that is the foundation for the tangibility of everyday reality. It is the experience of God, the Source, the Tao beyond description, but to be totally trusted.

If one were to think metaphorically of spirituality as a mountain of consciousness, religion is one way to climb up that mountain for some people. Level 4 is a primary method for understanding what the mountain is and accelerate the climb up it by willingly participating in the essence of that mountain: "Values" as "Being." That is true whether you are a religious person or not. If you are a religious person, Level 4 will help your consciousness/spirituality authenticate and expedite your progress up the mountain of spiritual understanding.

Why?

Values. To not merely parrot the words describing values, or quote holy scripture, or even to declare fealty to values, but rather to embody those values, is to understand the message of religious prophets and accordingly demonstrate true understanding of the spirit of their message, not just the letter of those messages.

After all, what were Jesus, Buddha, Krishna, Lao Tzu, Gandhi, Mother Teresa, Saint Francis, all guiding humanity to practice in our process of life? Values! Which values? Love, selflessness, forgiveness, humility, gratitude, integrity, compassion, wisdom, and many more. What are all of these? Values.

Therefore, the heart of spirituality, which is the purpose of any authentic religious practice, is to be an exemplification of such values, and thus Level 4.

I believe that most people fall into one of four categories:

1. Religious and spiritual (Level 4 consciousness)

2. Religious, but not spiritual (dogmatic) (Level 3 consciousness)

3. Spiritual, but not religious (Level 4 consciousness)

4. Not religious, Not spiritual (Level 3 consciousness)

If you think about it, we judge other people to be holy, spiritual, enlightened. How do we come to think of them in that way? Because they consistently, naturally, and authentically give us an experience of values. They are personifications of love, compassion, forgiveness, and sacrifice. Therefore values are the language of spirituality, and Level 4 is a commitment to practice personifying those values. Accordingly, people who operate from Level 4, and therefore embody and practice personifying their core values, are generally viewed to be spiritually advanced and as teachers and as people that others want to be around.

Imagine for a moment that mountain of consciousness has different elevations with different eco-zones of awareness. This mountain of consciousness is synonymous with the mountain of spirituality. At the top of the mountain is the connection point to the universe, to the Source, to Divinity, to God. And the higher you are on the mountain, the farther you see of that mountain as well as the landscape it dominates all around it. Only at the top of the mountain can you see the whole mountain, as well as the sky above that mountain and the earth surrounding it, and the oceans surrounding it and the entire universe and how it is all connected to Divinity, who created it.

That mountain, however, is not religion. Religion and spirituality are different, but related. Spirituality is the mountain; the reason for religion to exist is as one path up that mountain. Religion is one way of ascending the mountain of spirituality, but not the only way (in my opinion, anyway).

There is a western and eastern half to this mountain. The western half has the Western religions as broad pathways leading up the mountain with thick forests in between. These patterns include Judaism, Christianity, Islam and several more. The eastern side of the mountain contains Hinduism, Buddhism, Taoism, Shintoism, Jains, and others. Most people throughout history have chosen to walk one of these paths up the mountain.

However, in today's world, more and more people are leaving those well-worn paths and wandering around the mountain to explore other paths up the mountain. They're sometimes going through thick forests where they're discovering ways up the mountain on their own. They are exploring religious paths that are different from the one they were scripted into thinking was the only one. And whether they take one of the religious paths straight up the mountain or decide to break trail and make their own way up the mountain without following a religious path, it is all the same mountain leading to the same altitude to the same universal truth, created by the same creator.

How could it be any other way if it leads to God and God is the creator of everything?

This can seem like a blasphemous perspective to the dogmatic person, because of the Level 3 within that person. The ego, or Level 3, needs validation for its choices to think of itself as right, and therefore judges people disagreeing with those choices (such as having a different way to climb the mountain) as wrong. So, in essence, dogmatism and all of the suffering it has created in history (including religious wars and persecution) is an explainable Level 3 societal behavior with its roots in Level 3, which is actually adverse to the original teachings of the founders of those religions or systems of thought.

But what about selective (and selectively translated) statements picked out of statements by such founders? Here is one example: "Only through me do you come to the Father." What does that statement actually mean?

- Level 3 interprets it to be a single historical individual to whom you must commit unconditional belief in (Jesus), because the ego interprets it through the filter of individual ego-based reality (an individual person; the messenger of the message).

- Level 4 interprets it to be what that historically personified, embodied Messiah gave his life for (love, the message of the messenger). Level 4, therefore, may interpret it to mean, "Only through *Love* do you come to the Father, Who is the ultimate expression and experience of Love, and is Himself the Source of all Love."

Further, what does this mountain of consciousness have to do with Level 4? A person's Level 3 or Level 4 Identity not only determines that person's relative elevation on the mountain, it also determines his or her ascension up the mountain and at what speed that occurs. A person operating out of their Level 3 Identity tends to simply circle the mountain at the same elevation or stay in the relatively same place within their religious path. But a person at Level 4 is always progressing up the mountain, whether they are going straight up that mountain on one chosen religious path, or spiraling up the mountain exploring the connection between all of the paths of the mountain, and even the wilderness in between in terms of what they all share. It is this path that they all share that may be the most consistently representative of spiritual truth and which is most true.

POP QUIZ

Which of the four categories of spiritual/religious best fits you? What might help you climb the mountain better, faster, and with more passion going forward? Write down your answers.

LEVEL 4: EFFECTIVE RESPONSES
TO SUFFERING

The one thing you can't take away from me
is the way I choose to respond to what you do to me.
The last of one's freedoms is to choose one's attitude
in any given circumstance.
—*Viktor E. Frankl*

My awakening to my Level 4 Self began about one year before my son moved on from this incarnation. At this level of awareness I move beyond sadness, caused by the illusion of physical permanence, and feel grateful that my son and I crossed paths during this phase of an eternal journey.

There is no suffering for the Level 4 Self.

—*Chris Krupar*
Artist/Adventurer/Mortgage Lender

Imagine a man and his wife in a major metropolitan city walking down the street after an elegant dinner. The man is dressed in a tuxedo and the woman in a formal gown. It's raining lightly, and as they walk along under their umbrella, it's a perfect romantic evening, and they are now heading for their favorite concert.

They come across another man in a tuxedo who is on his hands and knees under a streetlight in the gutter looking for something. They stop and ask him, "What are you doing?"

He responds, "I've lost my car keys and I'm looking for them. Will you help me find them?"

They could hardly refuse him, so the strolling man gets down on his hands and knees and begins looking along with the first man for the car keys. Pretty soon it starts raining harder, his wife starts tapping her toe impatiently, and her husband asks a question of the guy they found in the gutter looking for the keys.

"My friend, we've spent ten minutes looking for your car keys and haven't found them. Our tuxedos are now ruined and we clearly aren't finding your car keys. Where exactly did you lose them?"

"Oh I lost them two blocks back, but the light is better here!" the man explained.

What does this story mean? It means that no matter how hard we look for something, if we are looking under the wrong "streetlight," we are not going to find what we're looking for. This is precisely the way to look at Level 3 versus Level 4 Identity.

We seek relief from the suffering and confusion and uncertainty in life, and if we are seeking to find the answers to those problems from our Level 3 Identity, we are looking under the wrong streetlight. What makes it the wrong streetlight is that the answers cannot be found through Level 3. No amount of temporary comfort, being more right than the next guy, or worldly validation is going to ultimately relieve the suffering in life.

Only the growth of consciousness can relieve suffering.

Level 4 Identity is the correct streetlight under which you will actually find your answers, your truth, your relief from suffering, your connection to meaning, your empowerment, your salvation, your "car keys."

Many holy ones have come throughout history to point us in the direction of the answers that we seek. These have included Krishna, Buddha, Lao Tzu, Christ, and even more current prophets such as Gandhi, Saint Teresa of Calcutta, and Saint Francis. The list includes hundreds of individuals throughout history, perhaps thousands. What was the universal message of these masters? I believe the message was that there are common values that connect us to the Source. Those values are recognized by all people in all cultures throughout history regardless of their belief systems intrinsic to those cultures. Some of these values include love, sacrifice, gratitude, selflessness, kindness, compassion, and charity.

Values, therefore, are the language of the larger, intangible reality from which we have eventuated. You may call that God, the Tao, the Source, Divinity, or the Universe. You may have still more names for it, but we all can sense the presence of that macro-intelligence benevolently guiding us forth.

In this world as a human being, suffering is a constant in everyone's life at some point or another. The Buddha recognized this and committed his life to overcoming it. Christ did the same. As did all the other holy ones throughout history. And what did they encourage us to do to alleviate suffering? They encouraged us to practice love, gratitude, reverence, integrity, truthfulness, and a host of other values.

These are all values, and therefore *values are the language of Divinity at our level of reality*. We intrinsically guide our own children using values as the parameters that they should operate within, even though we simultaneously recognize our hypocrisy because of our failure to live by values consistently. Oh, we may think that we do and say that we do, but how common is consistent and selfless behavior in human beings?

Suffering, therefore, is part of the perfection of the process to help us guide our way forward if we don't learn lessons through our cognitive abilities and karmic experiences created by our Level 3 Identity. Suffering is universally, eventually experienced, and accordingly deeply unsettling and unbalancing to human beings, who have the consciousness to try to understand and overcome it, but fail to through Level 3.

Level 3 Identity is the realm of suffering. After all, you can only be hurt if there is a you that you are trying to protect, in the individualistic and physical sense. But if you are Level 4 in your identity, the suffering disappears because at Level 4 it no longer matters. Why does the suffering no longer matter at Level 4?

Because, at Level 4 (as an identity that is undifferentiated, meaning that you are everything and not just your physical identity), you experience that you are the Universe that has created the perfection of its design. As a being that is now merged into the Universe, the Source, God consciousness, you now have a perspective that allows for change to occur at the physical level without the natural suffering that a Level 3 ego must experience. In addition, you have a larger view of the holistic connection of all things in time and space, so you don't personalize experiences and assign them judgment of worth within the duality paradigm as the only legitimate model of valuation.

In other words, you don't demonize uncomfortable experiences simply because they are uncomfortable (Level 3); you recognize them as necessary to the overall evolution of consciousness that must occur. The pendulum of the duality of tangible reality (right/wrong, heaven/hell, good/bad, comfortable/uncomfortable) is now recognized as intrinsic to evolution from Level 4 and is expanded beyond the need of mere comfort or animalistic survival. Your Soul, or true Self, accepts the perfection of all events that happen within the universe of consciousness by design. The ability to see this—to believe this, to know this—is the purest measure of a person's faith.

Faith is the conscious vesting of belief in that which is not guaranteed. It is an act of courage, a decision to trust and truly own the belief in the existence of the intangible, the existence of an intelligent force of energy that is benevolently guiding the perfection of it all by design.

But until we arrive at that Level 4 Identity with consistency, we need tools at Level 3 to be able to access our inner peace and our Level 4. The following is one of those tools that I have developed just for that purpose. It is a tool that is holistic, rather than surgical.

If, in moments of darkness in your life or in the life of someone you care about, you experience suffering, practice the following tool and see what shift of state occurs for you as a result.

REBALANCING PROCESS IN RESPONSE TO DARK PERSONAL REALITY

The process for overcoming suffering is one of taking a broad approach, including many different tools. This process involves, in general order, awareness, biochemistry, cognitive correction, emotional rebalancing, spirituality, and actions.

Awareness means to be objectively aware of where you're starting from. It means to consider your state of mind and whether it is above 5 on a scale of 1 to 10, or below that number. In awareness, it is important to be highly objective about how you have felt over a period of time, not just at any given instant. Generally, the rest of these tools will be used to respond to a negative reading on awareness.

Biochemistry means to look objectively and honestly at your capacity to be happier at this moment. This can be impacted by everything from outside chemicals (alcohol, tobacco, drugs) to sleep habits, to exercise habits, to walks in nature, to internal chemical imbalances. If a person's biochemistry is off, it can be almost impossible to feel better.

Therefore, biochemistry is the first place to look when a person is not happy.

Cognitive correction is a process brilliantly laid out by Dr. David Burns in his landmark book, *Feeling Good: The New Mood Therapy.* In the cognitive corrective process, a person goes through four specific steps to overcome unhappiness, founded on the premise that emotions are created by thoughts. In this process, the first step is to notice the emotion being felt. The second step is to recognize the automatic thoughts underlying the creation of that emotion. The third step is to categorize the automatic thought in one or more of ten cognitive distortions that Dr. Burns has identified as being common patterns that create dark thinking and depression. The fourth, and last step, involves a rational response where one looks at the situation from on high, as though from an outsider's perspective or even God's perspective.

Emotions refers to the next step in this process, which involves identifying the primary negative emotion being experienced, considering what the opposite emotion for that state would be, and then looking at the situation as though from that opposite emotional state that happens to be positive and contrary to the initial starting state. Doing this allows the instant recognition and experience of just how much control we have over our perception of reality if we remember our choice of filter or mental model to view (and accordingly act on) any given situation, even negatively perceived ones.

Spirituality refers to the process of getting in touch with one's connection to their Source, however one defines that Source. The Source is identified by many names: God, Jesus, Yahweh, the Tao, the Universe, Divinity, the Source. To reconnect to one's Source is a critical step in remembering our larger identity as a contrasting foundation to whom we think we are. This contrast is generally a choice between ego and the values or Soul. When treating ourselves as our ego, we will naturally operate from a defensive and smaller perspective than when treating or viewing ourselves as our values or Soul, which allows us to see situations from a larger and longer-term perspective. This spirituality rebalancing also, perhaps, invites an actual interface and participation from that Source into the problem, and more importantly into the solution.

Action, the last step in this overall process, is to initiate action from these rebalanced and empowered states. This action should be a reflection of one's new awareness, cognitive correction process, emotional rebalancing, spiritual identification and connection, all as foundations to revealing new options of action that may mitigate the situation. Whether, in fact, the situation is indeed mitigated, the individual practicing this methodology will instantly and dramatically feel differently about the situation, and perhaps more importantly see new options of response from a larger and more grounded place.

This multistep process is well grounded in the experience of psychologists, psychiatrists, ministers, therapists, and coaches throughout the world. It is a large and multifaceted and complete process to redefining one's interpretation and experience of reality, and therefore it impacts that reality in a very literal and real way.

Here is an example of a case study in how to practice this tool:

Situation: I feel depressed due to my fear of my economic future being so uncertain at my current job.

Awareness rebalancing: I am a 3 out of 10 in terms of how positive or light I am feeling at this time and over the past few weeks.

Biochemistry rebalancing: I am probably drinking a little too much at night and need to stop all alcohol for at least a month to see if I sleep better. I also need to start taking a thirty-minute walk every day (especially in nature) and start taking some vitamins. I need to be patient and do these new activities for a few weeks before I'll probably have the biochemical capacity to be as happy as I am committed to becoming.

Cognitive correction rebalancing:

- Emotion: I am feeling depressed.

- Automatic thought: I am so afraid that my boss doesn't like me and may fire me at any moment, and if he does that, I'll lose everything and be ruined!

- Cognitive distortion: My automatic thought is an example of being a *fortune teller* (which projects fearsome futures without enough information) and *emotional reasoning* (which has me think that it must be true because I am feeling like it is true, which isn't necessarily objectively true). [Note: Dr. Burns has identified ten common cognitive distortions that typify dark thoughts leading to depression and suicide, and these are just some examples. Read his book for all ten.]

- Rational response: Well, when I look at my situation objectively, my real value at this job (or any job) is how much value I add to the situation, and that is both my opportunity as well as my responsibility. I'm committed to accepting that responsibility and giving everything I have to the job, and that is all I can do. If I do that, this boss will see the value or the next boss will, but either way, I can only control what I can influence so I'm going to focus there rather than waste time with worry. After that, it is all up to God anyway.

Emotional rebalancing: I am feeling depressed and afraid. What are the opposite emotional states from these? Happy and courageous. What would happy be thinking about my situation right now? What would courageous be doing right now in my situation?

Spiritual rebalancing: I believe in Jesus Christ being who He said He was (or whomever I see as my access point to Divinity), and I believe He is with me at all times. That includes this situation, so I will trust Him to guide me and protect me from harm, and while doing my part to improve the situation, I will trust where it leads as His will.

Actions: I will review all of the rebalancing approaches every day, several times a day, and execute a course of action that reflects those new perspectives to the very best of my abilities as of this moment. I will take the following actions in each of the above areas and start by doing the following (write your responses in your journal).

POP QUIZ

What do you do when you feel blue, depressed, dark, or negative? Do you fight it and overcome it somehow? Are you willing to take the responsibility for your own thoughts, if doing so would eliminate your suffering? Write down your answers.

6

LEVEL 4: LARGER IMPLICATIONS FOR LEVEL 3 VERSUS LEVEL 4 IN THE WORLD

When you operate at Level 4 Identity, you are operating as your true Self, your Soul. That Soul goes beyond this lifetime in both directions in time. When you are operating from Level 4 (your Soul), you unlock a secret chamber that reveals who you really are and why you are really here.

Most people go through life and only periodically find the chamber open, like when they fall in love. When they have children. When they feel great compassion for a stranger and help that stranger. But these are seen as just part of the flow of events within the world Level 3 inhabits.

> **The secret chamber to true understanding of the Soul is locked and needs to be unlocked with a code. That code is the core values that you awaken and begin to personify in your thoughts, intentions, and actions. That code is practicing your Level 4 Identity.**

If you notice the people in history who have gone through dramatic spiritual transformations, whether you look at Buddha, Gandhi, Christ, and Saint Francis, for example, these individuals all awakened to a larger sense of power and connection to Divinity as they committed their lives to personifying values.

Therefore, values and their personification on a consistent basis is what opens the vault to your Soul and allows you to live the life that you came here to live.

Unfortunately most people miss this opportunity. Why? Because most people don't even know that there is a secret chamber, much less how to unlock it with intentionality.

In 1968 I was sixteen years old. I made a bet for $10 with my dad that the world wouldn't survive until 1974. The Vietnam War was raging, and America was in turmoil. Black hated white, women hated men, young hated old. It all looked like it was over for the world. I, like most of my generation, had grown up practicing huddling under our desks in case the Russians fired nuclear bombs at our country. How could the world possibly survive another six years, I asked myself.

My dad took the bet. I asked him why. He described a life where he was born into a poor family in 1913. He had six brothers and sisters and his mom died when he was five years old giving birth to still another child. His father worked on a coal wagon. He would come home every day with his hands bleeding from the sharp coal, and his loving Irish wife would wrap his hands in cloth to stop the bleeding and prepare for the next day.

As previously discussed earlier in this book, his mom died, his dad died a month later of "a broken heart" (obviously, alcoholism, we were Irish, as you know). My dad and all of his siblings were sent off to various orphanages in Troy, New York, in 1918. When he was finally old enough to get out of that hellish place (where he was often punished severely for the slightest infraction), it was 1931. The Great Depression was under way and there were no jobs. After that came World War II. My dad explained that his earliest memories were of people declaring that the world was going to end from the poison gas being used in World War I, and his whole life people had been telling him that the world was going to end due to WWI, the Great Depression, The Second World War, the atom bomb—and it never did. Therefore, my dad stopped believing the world was ever going to end, and so did I. (He won the bet, obviously.)

I think this same tendency of "doom and gloom" interpretations for apocalyptic end-of-the-world scenarios are part of many religions as well, which further feeds the Level 3 ego's need to protect itself from such devastation. "Perhaps if I am a believer in the right path, the right religion, I won't be destroyed like everyone else when the apocalypse finally comes," seems to be the perspective for many Level 3 people.

Like Jim Morrison of the musical group The Doors said, "Nobody gets out alive." Clearly, we know that we all die physically, but does that mean that "I" die, the real "I"? So, if that is recognized, what would an apocalypse matter even if it ever did happen? We are all temporary as physical beings anyway, right? So, clearly, the only true salvation is the salvation of awareness of our larger, eternal Self that exists beyond the limitations of our physical selves and our worldly personalities and egos. We aren't allowed, yet, to fully understand what that exactly is, but can experience it nonetheless. And the access point to that experience is found in Level 4 Identity.

What's the point? The point is that the world, as long as humans have been in it, has experienced suffering and drama. And that is not going to change except over time with the evolution of consciousness.

The evolution of consciousness is the path forward toward the realization of the divine nature within us as humans. When we are in that place, there will be no more hatred or wars or suffering. But there will be plenty of all of those until we arrive at that place.

It is not the invitation of suffering that really matters. It is the experience of suffering—or not. Level 3 Identity, which is where 90 percent of humanity has lived 98 percent of its life, is the arena of suffering. This was precisely the mission of Buddha. He sought to fully understand the reason for suffering and how to eradicate it in a person's life. His resulting enlightenment created a great spiritual tradition in the world that thrives to this day.

But that was all 2,500 years ago. Some 2,000 years ago another prophet of God appeared. Jesus had a ministry of the heart. His ministry was essentially one of love, forgiveness, and sacrifice. As Jesus demonstrated with his life as a lesson for the rest of us, we give our most effective teaching to others by who we are, and he was all of those things.

What are all of those things? Values that are personified in everyday activity. And what is that?

That is the Level 4 Identity within you, and me, and everyone on the planet with reasonably healthy mental capacity. That is the secret code within us, the God seed, the crystal that is the crucible within us of our own divine nature that awakens the pathway out of suffering.

What, then, are the implications of evolving from Level 3 Identity to Level 4 Identity for the world as a whole?

A world that lives in the flow and harmony of values in a natural way and in doing so rarely experiences any form of suffering. And that may just be "the kingdom of heaven within you."

In 1976 I was a twenty-four-year-old seeker of truth. I found myself sitting on a cliff with a Holy Man from India one July day that year. I was going through a sacred ceremony with him when he told me a profound series of truths. He asked me to live my life by three sacred truths, and I agreed to his request, even though I didn't yet know what they were and therefore what I was promising to *do* and *be*.

As we sat on the edge of the cliff and he guided me through various mystical and secret rituals that go back thousands of years, he shared the three truths with me. I'm now sharing them with you. I decided to live my life around these, and you will have that opportunity as well.

The first truth of the Holy Man was this:

Doubt is the source of all suffering.

I found that was an interesting idea so, before discussing the other two truths, let me tell you what happened. I went home that night and was alone. I decided to write a letter to Nancy. Nancy was a girl I had fallen for deeply and had left me for another guy named Robert. I wrote her a letter that night that basically absolved her of any responsibility or guilt in the breakup of our relationship. I wished her well and forgave all that needed to be forgiven and sealed the envelope. On the back of the envelope for some strange reason, I decided to write the first truth of the Holy Man and wrote, "Doubt is the source of all suffering." I probably did it so she could be reminded that she should have no doubt about going forward without me, but I honestly don't remember why actually. (It was over forty years ago, after all.)

So I sent the letter, and two weeks later I got a phone call at night from her boyfriend. He was calling me to, of all things, thank me for saving his life.

I asked him how I could have possibly saved his life, given that I'd never met him before. He explained to me that he had had a Smith & Wesson .38 Special in his mouth five minutes earlier and was squeezing the trigger to commit suicide. His eyes happened to fall on the coffee table where an envelope lay. He read the quote on the back of the envelope, "Doubt is the source of all suffering."

Those profound words made him put the gun down and keep it down for good. That seemed like a mystical moment validating the great first truth.

I realize the profundity of this truth. If doubt is the source of all suffering, then whatever the opposite of doubt is must clearly be the antidote to suffering. What is the opposite of doubt? Faith! Faith in yourself, faith in the world, faith in other people, faith in Divinity, faith in all of it. Faith is the vesting of belief in that which is not tangibly guaranteed. It's a courageous act. And when we exercise it, we are choosing, through our free will, to see the world through a lens of positive outcomes, rather than what our ego/emotional limbic brain and primitive brain survival instinct has us gravitate to in fear and negative possibilities projected from our fearful mind.

Since our experience of outcomes is judged by whether that experience is positive or negative, faith is actually a tool to be used to eradicate suffering. It expands the perspective to a big enough context that whatever happened no longer matters in the way that it did before we expanded our perspective or expanded our consciousness.

Back to the cliff with the Holy Man. The Holy Man went on to explain the second truth:

Everybody is doing the best they can with what they have to work with all of the time, and your job is not to judge them or fix them, but give them more to work with, and they will take it from there.

This truth had me realize that my first tendency when it came to other people was judgment. That judgment was undoubtedly based in trying to discern whether they were a validation of what I thought reality was and should be, or a challenge to that perspective. It moved me from this judgmental tendency to compassion. Because I realized that everyone is doing the best they know how to, but they need more to work with in terms of knowledge and information and guidance so that they can do better in the future in achieving results that help them along their path.

Also, this put me into alignment with what the holy ones have been saying from all traditions about being responsible for yourself without judging others. "Judge not lest ye be judged," said Christ.

The third truth the Holy Man shared was, in some ways, the hardest one to accept. He said:

Everything in life and the Universe is always and already perfect, just as it is. It is only our limited perspective that causes us to experience any of it as suffering.

Wait a minute! How could that possibly be true? What about babies who get leukemia? What about the Jews who died in Hitler's death camps? "How could that be perfect?" I asked myself. But looking at the third truth carefully over the last forty years, I've come to conclude that it is actually the truest of all three.

The third truth has a subtle secret within it. It essentially gives us the pathway that this book is encouraging you to pursue: the choice of your perspective as your guidance system to creating what you want in life. In the second part of this truth, the statement that suffering is a result of limited perspective invites the obvious approach to changing that limited perspective into an expanded one if we wish to have a different experience than suffering.

For example, with babies who have leukemia, one perspective in the world might be a Christian perspective that sees that this world is not the one that ultimately matters anyway, but rather heaven does, and that is the eternal destination we are seeking. Accordingly, while the example of babies with leukemia creates a suffering experience for those babies and all who love them, the Christian believes that such suffering is temporary and will be replaced by an experience of eternal bliss in heaven, and therefore is acceptable despite the human-level experience of suffering.

From a Buddhist perspective, we each choose our lives to learn specific lessons as well as burn off old karma in an inexorable climb up the mountain of consciousness, until we realize our inevitable enlightenment somewhere in the future. Even from a quantum physics perspective, when one considers the scope of time and space, anything that happens at this plane of existence is relatively insignificant to the overall perfection of design.

Light, for example, travels something like 6.4 trillion miles per year. That's 6.4 million×1 million. It takes 100,000 of those years just to get across our galaxy, the Milky Way, from one end to the other. Imagine! And they currently believe there are between 200 and 400 billion galaxies in the universe. Those are just the ones that we currently can find. So, in all fairness, with the multidimensionality of quantum physics going into the micro world and Newtonian physics exploring the edges of an ever-expanding apparent universe, how important are the singular events to our little lives on planet earth, which last but a few decades amidst such eternity?

You don't need to believe any of these truths are truth. You may believe some of them are true and others not. But I promise you this, if you follow through on the invitations of this book with sincerity and resolve, you will realize your Level 4 Identity, and you will have a future unlimited by the past. Further, you will significantly advance your place on the mountain of consciousness. And if you are a Christian, Buddhist, Jew, or any other formal religion, you will now be a significantly more authentic version of that belief system.

Your relationships will transform, along with your health, along with your fulfillment in your occupation. You will answer questions you may have had your whole life, and now be able to provide yourself those answers, along with sharing those answers with other people.

POP QUIZ

How would your life change if you operated every day with awareness and practice of the three truths? Write down your answers.

7

YOUR DECISION AND
PATH FORWARD

*Old as I am in age, I have no feeling that I have ceased to
grow inwardly or that my growth will stop at the dissolution
of the flesh. What I am concerned with is my readiness to
obey the call of truth, my God, from moment to moment, no
matter how inconsistent it may appear. My commitment is
to truth, not to consistency.*

—Mahatma Gandhi

What you perceive you believe. What you believe is based upon either an active or passive relationship with external reality. If you have a passive relationship with external reality (which Level 3, ego-based identities do), then you merely allow circumstances to create reactions from you that form scripts that end up defining your identity and reality, and experience in life, and therefore the quality of your life.

But, at Level 4 Identity, you create an active relationship with life and impact your power and experiences within that life accordingly. To literally view yourself and your thoughts and your actions and your intentions through the filter of your core values is to actively redefine the patterns of your life and their consequences as an active influencer to them, through assuming the responsibility and opportunity of a Level 4 life.

When you redefined the patterns of your life through this process at Level 4 of value filtration, you end up creating a new kaleidoscope of informational experiences that allows a more whole and complete view beyond the limited judgments and opinions of a Level 3 scripting. When you move beyond the limitations of Level 3 scripting, you move beyond the confines of the ego that conscripts your identity and makes your primary priority your physical survival and social image only, in favor of a more noble and bright purpose to your existence.

As you ascend the mountain of consciousness to your Level 4 Identity, even for a few moments, you change your perception and therefore your activities within any subsequent experience in response to it. When you do that, you *become* an expression of values and you always tilt the situation toward the light rather than the darkness.

Suffering that occurs in karma as a consequence of poor actions is illuminated when operating from Level 4. And even when the greatest experiences of suffering occur (for example, death of a loved one or even your own terminal disease), which naturally create the invitation to suffering, the Level 4 Identity person is largely immune to any actual suffering due to the scope of their perspective. It is as if they are now standing on a large barge on a wavy ocean rather than a little rowboat.

Inner peace is the result of Level 4 Identity, where isolation and suffering amid periodic experiences of happiness is the pathway of the Level 3 Identity.

Which destiny are you going to choose?

I would like to finish this book by sharing with you perhaps my favorite spiritual story.

Four old monks were living in a forest in a monastery. They have lived their whole lives there and had very successful lives as devoted monks. Their monastery is well-known, and they loved having people from the town come to attend services, which had fulfilled their life commitments of spiritual support for others.

But as the years went by, time changed things and the monks were now getting older and the monastery was falling into disrepair. There were fewer people coming to services as a result, and the old monks were worried about what was going to happen to the monastery after they died, which wouldn't be too distant into the future.

There happened to be a Jewish mystic who periodically visited the forest and lived in a cave nearby. Somehow, the monks always seemed to know when he was in the forest.

The three junior monks asked the senior monk to go and visit the Jewish mystic to see if he had any answers for what bothered them relative to the continuation of the monastery after they were all gone.

So he went to the cave. He found the Jewish mystic. He explained the situation to the old mystic, who responded simply with, "I have no idea what you should do." This was terribly discouraging to the old monk, but with resignation he turned to leave the cave. Just as he was exiting the cave, the old Jewish mystic called out one last comment to him. "While I don't know what you should do about the monastery, I do know that one of you is the Messiah."

"What did you just say?" asked the old monk from the door of the cave.

"I said that one of you is the Messiah," the mystic repeated.

As the monk walked back to the monastery, he ruminated on the mystic's message. He thought to himself, "Could it be Bob? I doubt it because Bob is angry all the time, but maybe that's the way the Messiah decided to show up this time around."

He continued the analysis as he walked. "I wonder if it's Fred? But Fred is awfully quiet all the time. Maybe he decided to be a quieter Messiah this time around."

Upon returning to the monastery, he shared with the other monks what the Jewish mystic had told him. "He said that one of us is the Messiah."

All the monks were confused by this and went through a similar process of rumination that the old monk had been doing on his walk back from the cave. They each wondered which one of them was the Messiah. As a result, they thought they better cover their bases and assume that any one of them could be the Messiah, so they began to treat each other as though they were each the potential Messiah, with great reverence and love and care. They also realized that the monastery needed to be attended to and that the Messiah would probably expect that if they were living there as monks, so they began to apply extra energy in weeding the gardens, painting the monastery, and fixing the place up.

As a result of the monks' attendance to the monastery, people began to return to services, as well as returning to the renewed spirit with which the old monks seemed to practice the sacred rituals of their order. Even a few young people asked about possibly becoming a monk and wondered if they could come and live there.

So what is the point of the story?

The point of the story is that, like the monks at the monastery, we tend to focus on strategic and tactical solutions to what we see before us, but if we believe that we are operating with a more pure and loving and enlightened force watching over our activities, we will often change the pattern of those activities and give more than we thought we had to give. We will begin to treat everyone as potentially the "Messiah" with great reverence and love, which has them treat us in the same way. In fact, we save the "monastery" of our lives and our world through our mindful reverence and loving actions in honor of a holy presence in our midst.

Therefore, consider that you in your life are in something that is the equivalent of a monastery. See everyone else as potentially being the Messiah. In other words, see other people as their Level 4 values that you must treat with great reverence and respect. By doing this, you yourself will begin to live in alignment with your own values and Level 4 Identity. And by doing all of this, you will save the monastery.

The monastery is, in fact, the world around us. May you be courageous and bold on your path of practicing the largest version of you as your gift to the world. Because, in the end, your life is a gift from God, and what you do with it is your gift back to God. Do that from the highest place within you, and you will have a very rewarding final conversation with yourself when you have five minutes left on your deathbed.

You will not have wasted the gift.

If you follow through on evolving and awakening your Level 4 Identity, and you remember and practice your Personal Life Vision along with the three truths of the Holy Man, you will look back on this experience as a validation of what you hoped life could turn out to be.

I know because it has happened for me, and I am the last one who ever believed that he deserved that it could. Please do for yourself what I was fortunate enough to have happen to me.

As our journey draws to a close together, I will reiterate what I said at the end of my first book, which is this: I realize that this book is not written perfectly, but please know that it was intended perfectly, as an expression of my Level 4 Identity inviting your Level 4 Identity forth, because in the end, they are not two separate places—as you and I are not two separate beings—when in that sacred place.

Namaste.

A lot of people are waiting for Martin Luther King

or Mahatma Gandhi to come back,

but they are gone.

We are it.

It is up to us.

It is up to you.

—*Marian Wright Edelman*

And who you *are* creates what you *do*,

and what *you* do creates your impact on the world,

and therefore, impacts not only your destiny…

but the destiny of the whole world.

ACKNOWLEDGMENTS

This book is dedicated to all humanity, and the future it is capable of if it chooses to use this information to move to a collective Level 4 Identity (which will save and optimize it), versus continuing to live at Level 3, which will surely destroy it.

And, of course, to all those sacred Souls along my journey who have co-created this book by the impact they have had on my personal life. That particularly includes my life partner and wife, Reese, and my incredible sons, Cameron and Holden. It also includes the rest of my family, friends, clients through the years, and all the mentors who have supported me along the way. May their influence on the world, and yours for that matter, be as profound as my journey has invited me to be on my humble path—as I continue to "stumble toward enlightenment."

ABOUT THE AUTHOR

Al Killeen

B.A. (cum laude); C.M.L.; C.M.T.

Killeen Development Technologies
Integrative Mastery Programs

Founder/President

Integrative Training in Leadership/Management/
Coaching in Business & Life

Al Killeen has spent the last fifty years studying the human condition applied to life, relationships and business, through the perspectives of a broad spectrum of traditions. His résumé includes original work toward being a European Intellectual History Professor and toward becoming a Zen Monk. That was followed by a career in Pharmaceuticals, Finance, the Mortgage Industry (25 years), and ultimately a Business/Life Mastery Trainer (18 years). He has been the Founder/President of Highline-Equitrust Mortgage Corporation (10 years, sold at a 6,000% profit over starting capital), President of the Colorado Mortgage Lenders Association (1997-98), Founder/Inaugural President of the

Rocky Mountain Mortgage Lenders Association (1997-98; an 8 state alliance of mortgage associations), and the Ethics Chairman for the CMLA (1995). He is currently the Founder/CEO and President of Killeen Development Technologies and Integrative Mastery Programs (18 years).

Al has successfully trained integrative Leadership, Management and Coaching skills to hundreds of individuals and organizational executives in dozens of major companies (including both Wells Fargo and Re/Max) using the tools and technologies of Integrative Mastery Programs. He considers this to be among the greatest areas of fulfillment and accomplishment of his life. His compelling first book: *Soul Proprietorship: 8 Critical Steps to Overcoming Problems in Business and Life* was published in December 2009.

Clients include Fortune 500 companies (Wells Fargo, Re/Max, Medtonic), as well as many privately owned firms. Individual clients include dozens of CEOs, "C" level Executives, managers at all levels, 4th generation owner of largest privately-owned Department Store chain in America, and an NFL Quarterback.

Author of 2 books (*Soul Proprietorship: 8 Critical Steps to Overcoming Problems in Business and Life*, 2009; *Soul Experience: The 4th Level of Identity*, 2018)

Al's areas of focus include writing books, keynote speeches (International/domestic), training workshops, executive and personal Mastery Programs, guiding Spiritual retreats, and coaching in the areas of Integrative Leadership, Management and Coaching for:

ORGANIZATIONS

- Mortgage Lending / Real Estate professionals
- Sales organizations / Financial organizations

- "Enlightened Leadership" organizations; Boards of Directors
- Service and Technology organizations
- Consultants, Business Coaches and Business Teams

INDIVIDUALS

- Executives (CEOs, CFOs, COOs, Senior Management)
- Sales professionals
- Career enhancement
- Spiritual development
- Life balance
- Spousal relations
- Entrepreneurs
- Individuals desiring integrated empowerment and mastery of life

SERVICES

- Individual Programs for Integrative Mastery
- Organizational Programs for Organizational/Cultural Transformation
- Personal Coaching
- Executive Business Coaching
- International and Domestic Keynote Speeches

- Workshops

- Retreats

- Tools for empowered and effective business and life actualization

- Books, audios and videos to support effectiveness

CURRENT PRACTICE OVERVIEW

- 50+ individual, Senior Executive, long-term coaching clients

- Current average Coaching client engagement = 9.3 years

- 22 companies which operate regionally and nationally in mortgage lending, real estate, banking, engineering, food services, consulting, manufacturing, and technology in seven different industries in eleven states and Canada

- 18,000+ hours of Personal/Professional Coaching of hundreds of executives

- 18 years in top 3 percent of Professional Business Coaches internationally

- Registered and authorized Vistage Speaker (largest international CEO support organization in the world; 114 speeches to over 1,700 CEOs/Senior Executives)

- MBA Mentor: Leeds Business School—University of Colorado

RECOMMENDED READING (OR LISTENING)

Soul Proprietorship: The 8 Critical Steps to Overcoming Problems in Business and Life, Al Killeen

3 Pillars of Zen, Roshi Phillip Kapleau
A General Theory of Love, Lewis/Amini and Lannon
A Guide for the Advanced Soul: A Book of Insight, Susan Hayward
A New Earth: Awakening To Your Life's Purpose, Eckhart Tolle
A Simple Path, Mother Teresa
Authentic Happiness, Martin Seligman
Autobiography of a Yogi, Paramhamsa Yogananda
Awaken the Giant Within, Anthony Robbins
Be Here Now, Ram Dass
Big Magic: Creative Living Beyond Fear, Elizabeth Gilbert
Black Elk Speaks, John G. Neihardt
Change Your Thoughts, Change Your Life, Dr. Wayne Dyer
Face the Fear... And Do It Anyway, Susan Jeffers
Feeling Good: The New Mood Therapy, David D. Burns MD
Flow: The Psychology of Optimal Experience, Mihaly Csikszentimhalyi
Further Along the Road Less Travelled, M. Scott Peck
Gandhi: An Autobiography, Gandhi
Grist for the Mill, Ram Dass
How to Meditate: A Practical Guide to Making Friends with Your Mind, Pema Chödrön
Jesus: A Pilgrimage, James Martin

Journey to Ixtlan, Carlos Castaneda

Leadership and the New Science, Margaret Wheatley

Learned Optimism, Martin Seligman

Lessons from the Light, Dr. Kenneth Ring

Letting Go: The Pathway of Surrender, David R. Hawkins M.D. Ph.D.

Make Me an Instrument of Your Peace, Kent Nerburn

Man's Search for Meaning, Viktor Frankl

Markings, Dag Hammarskjold

Memories, Dreams, Reflections, Carl Jung

Overcoming Addictions (The Spiritual Solution), Deepak Chopra

Paths to God: Living the Bhagavad Gita, Ram Dass

Plato, Not Prozak, Lou Marinoff

Polishing the Mirror: How to Live from Your Spiritual Heart, Ram Dass

Power vs. Force, David Hawkins

Quiet Your Mind, John Selby

Real Power (Business Lessons from the Tao Te Ching), Autry & Mitchell

Richest Man in Babylon, George Clason

Siddhartha, Herman Hesse

St. Francis, G.K. Chesterton

Stumbling Toward Enlightenment, Geri Larkin

The 7 Habits of Highly Effective People, Stephen Covey

The Alchemist, Paulo Coelho

The Art of Happiness, The Dalai Lama

The Bible, King James Version

The Book of Chuang Tzu, Chuang Tzu

The Complete Works of Lao Tzu, Hua-Ching Ni

The Consolation of Philosophy, Boetheus

The Divine Matrix, Gregg Braden

The Doors of Perception, Aldous Huxley

The Enchiridion, Epictetus

The Fifth Discipline, Peter Senge

The Four Agreements, Don Miguel Ruiz

The Gnostic Gospel of Saint Thomas, Tau Malachi

The I-Ching: Chinese Book of Changes, Wu Wei

The Inner Game of Tennis, W. Timothy Gallway

The Path of Least Resistance, Robert Fritz

The Phenomenon of Man, Pierre Teilhard de Chardin

The Power of Intention, Dr. Wayne Dyer

The Prophet, Kahlil Gibran

The Road Less Travelled, M. Scott Peck

The Sage's Tao Te Ching: Ancient Advice for the Second Half of Life,
William Martin

The Tao of Physics, Fritjof Capra

The Tibetan Book of Living and Dying, Sogyal Rinpoche

The Twelve Conditions of a Miracle: The Miracle Worker's Handbook,
Todd Michael

The Ultimate Happiness Prescription: 7 Keys to Joy and Enlightenment,
Deepak Chopra

Think on These Things, J. Krishnamurti

Transcending the Levels of Consciousness: The Stairway to Enlightenment,
David R. Hawkins M.D. Ph.D.

Unlimited Power, Anthony Robbins

Where There is Light: New Expanded Edition, Paramahansa Yogananda

Why Bad Things Happen To Good People, Rabbi Harold Kushner

You Can Heal Your Life, Louise Hay

Zen and the Art of Motorcycle Maintenance, Robert Pirsig

Zen Mind, Beginner's Mind, Shunryu Suzuki

Zen to Go, Jon Winokur

ADDITIONAL TESTIMONIALS

One of the gifts of being coached by Mr. Al Killeen is becoming aware of the concept of a 4th level of Identity. Once you become aware, you instantly realize that you spend most of your time at Level 3, which almost always results in a less-than-satisfying experience, regardless of the situation or circumstances. After becoming aware of the 4th level, the next step is to practice "being there." It is certainly not easy at first. What is easy is to slip back and react from Level 3. **When you do enter the 4th level, the clarity and calm that you experience that replaces what would have been a "lack of clarity" and anxiety, is a wonderful experience.** *This applies to work situations as well as life at home with your family and loved ones.*

—Michael Landis
Mortgage Lender/Executive/Husband/Father

My awakening to my Level 4 Self began about one year before my son moved on from this incarnation. At this level of awareness, I move beyond sadness, caused by the illusion of physical permanence, and feel grateful that my son and I crossed paths during this phase of an eternal journey. **There is no suffering for the Level 4 Self.**

—Chris Krupar
Artist/Adventurer/Mortgage Lender

Through Al's teachings, I have experienced life at a whole new level. This book will help you rise above life's complications caused by stress, drama or imbalance. I learned through this book when I engage life at the "4th Level of Identity" I make a conscious choice through a disciplined habit which **results in a more accomplished, fulfilled and joyful life**.

Often times I hear people complain or brag about how their life is complicated. What Al teaches in this book is how to understand life at such a level where you can consciously overcome complications caused by stress, drama or imbalance.

Living life at the 4th level of identity creates simplicity coupled with all the rewards life has to offer.

Some books are intended to entertain; some books are intended to be experienced. The message in this book needs to be experienced. Allow yourself to become enrolled in the teachings of this book and you will experience a more accomplished, fulfilled and joyful life.

- *Living life at a Level 4 is a learned choice, continue with the choice and it becomes a habit.*

- *Life is complicated by our ego, simplified by our love.*

- ***Our Level 3 ego wants us to look important, Level 4 values allows us to be significant.***

- *We cannot always be in Level 4, however with the understanding of Level 4 we are aware when we are not.*

- Sometimes we bask in the ego's glory and we enjoy Level 3. There is nothing wrong with this because with the awareness of Level 4 we understand this is our choice.

- It is impossible for me to be a victim when I practice Level 4 Identity.

When the ego is silenced, patience is prominent
A patient mind is programed for accomplishment

—Jim Nunn
Executive/Husband/Father

1. Being aware of The 4th Level of Identity has removed so much needless pain and suffering from my life.

2. Making decisions from Level 4 Identity lightens my load. The decisions are more obvious and come from a deeper knowing.

3. Whether it is with customers or kids, I know I can speak clearly and have nothing to regret or apologize for later when coming from Level 4.

4. I am able to truly care about others when I am in Level 4 Identity and that has made a wonderful difference in my life.

5. When I notice that I am in Level 3, I defer all major decisions until I am firmly standing in Level 4. **Life seems to work with me when I come from Level 4**.

6. The beauty of Level 4 is that once you are aware of Level 4, you can never unknow it.

7. *When I am in my Level 4 Identity, the turbulence of life falls to the background and it feels like I am home.*

8. *Level 4 has helped me have a kinder and more stable relationship with myself.*

9. *My Level 4 is responsible for deleting my Level 3 emails before clicking "send."*

—**Kevin Francis**
Husband/Father/Business Owner

*I have been looking a lifetime for what Al called "Awakening the Paradise Within." **The 4th Level of Identity has changed the lens of my soul of what I see and how I react to the universe**. It presents a serenity that allows me to see the everyday miracles in all my individuality.*

—**Paul Martirano**
Father/Husband/Naval Officer (Ret.)

*Living more regularly from a Level 4 perspective is an authentic, **life-altering game changer**, void of the ego-based survival instinct, which has often held me back. My enlightened invitation to engage humanity from a higher and humbler place of Christian-inspired service, has produced immeasurable results in my relationships, my happiness, and how I view my true purpose in the world.*

—**Michael Ermish**
Husband/Father/Executive/Servant

*Al Killeen will guide you through the never-ending climb to the top of self-mastery by leading you to discover who you really are. Once you know who you are, and you are completely and totally honest with yourself, **you can begin to become*** *the person you want to be. During this journey you will see others in a new light, understanding their journey with no preconceptions of their thoughts, motives, or agendas.*

—Dustin Smoot
Husband/Executive/Adventurer

Al's book, Soul Experience: The 4th Level of Identity *is the perfect follow-up to his first book* Soul Proprietorship: 8 Critical Steps to Overcoming Problems in Business and Life. *It asks the questions that only you can answer and gives you permission to choose a life you know is possible.*

When I live my life at the 4th Level of Identity I become calm and clear. I feel stronger, more confident and my life becomes fulfilled. **I now operate from a perspective of love and light which can be an example for family, friends, employees and business associates.** *I highly recommend taking this personal reading challenge. It puts the "extra" in an ordinary life. You can do it.*

—Anthony Full
Grateful Husband, Proud Father, Enthusiastic Entrepreneur

Al's words invite you to explore your life's meaning. He encourages you to be present and aware while interacting with humanity using your unique talents and traits. **His revolutionary, values-based approach allows us to extend our limitless compassion to others while exceeding our own goals.**

—Corey Smith
Father/Husband/Learner/Mortgage Lender

Using these principals has transformed my life. **I have witnessed a remarkable, even enviable culture emerge in my organization.** *By operating from an Undifferentiated, Empowered, Values-Based Self, it has given others around* *me the safe space to bring their best selves forward. There is considerably less stress and anxiety in my life as well.*

Thank you, Al, for bringing this awareness into my life.

—Phil Shell
Husband/Father/Real Estate Executive Manager

The extraordinary relationship that I've had with Al over a number of years, has not only been a blessing for my soul, but has created an awareness of my Level 4 "Self" which encompasses the core values that my Personal Life Vision tries to live every day. Values like love, compassion and stewardship are personified at this identity.

True inner peace in all aspects of my life, and realizing the profound significance of relationship, happens when I engage life at my Level 4 existence. *It's when I toggle to the lower levels of Self, where challenges occur. It makes me realize how important the conscious choice to remain at this highest level truly is for my personal growth.*

Like anything worthwhile, this enlightened lifetime journey is a discipline that takes practice and awareness. In addition to my God-centered life, having Al's friendship and guidance along the way insures that I have a remarkable, abundant, and impactful life to live daily.

—Don Ziegler
Husband/Executive/Philanthropist/Entrepreneur

*My introduction to living in Level 4 came through a presentation with my business team. We all went away transformed forever. Living, managing, parenting, partnering and just being at **Level 4 is like having the fog clear and seeing what life is meant to be for oneself.** Everything is easier, there are always answers, it just feels* *right at Level 4. It's even better when the people in your life understand and live in Level 4 and you can support each other in this way of being.*

—Sue Melnick
Wife/Mother/Chief Operating and
Compliance Officer/Attorney

Level 4? I'm not sure I'm worthy of that level of identity, but I can say I've moved from ego-based goals to a more fulfilling ideal of striving to be a Good Samaritan by following the "Golden Rule" and putting it all into action!

My association with Al Killeen over the past 10 years has helped me form these ideals and more.

—John G. Olson
Insurance Agent/
Community Service Volunteer

Once you are aware and understand the peace from within at Level 4 from what most of us operate in at Level 3 you will work harder and commit to pursuing Level 4. **My journey towards being a more authentic and better version of myself has helped me get through some of the very best and worst moments with a greater understanding and purpose of who I am and how I am to react.** *My relationship with my brother Al Killeen has been life changing and I am blessed to be able to share my gift of gratitude with others.*

—Dwight Millard
Christian/Husband/Father/Mortgage Lending Manager

Al Killeen first introduced me to the 4 levels of identity many years ago, and it is a topic that we talk over often. It was an awakening that has forever changed my life. The concept of Level 4 Self reminds me to think about the bigger picture,

without my ego's input. It is a practice (and I say 'practice'
because I strive for it every day, and often times need reminders)
that allows me to be my purest form of authenticity and love.
When I am operating from my Level 4 non-ego-based
Self, my relationships are more fulfilling, my interactions
with colleagues and clients are more meaningful and my
heart/soul genuinely feel at peace with a purpose.

—Bradley Dusek
Husband/Father/Mortgage Lender

Learning to be in the Level 4 has **helped me turn the**
morale of my company around *and improve the way I*
am training with my staff.

—Thomas Starks
President /Owner/Father

The past two years have been very trying for me as mid-life
hurls down the alleyway of my experience including the
"bowling balls" (experiences) of aging and ill parents; sibling
disagreements over care; raising a teen; operating multiple
businesses… just to name a few. As a human, my default
hardwiring is to reel on the heels of egocentric overwhelm.
When I wake to the universal truth that every decision
is choice between Level 3 or Level 4 Identity, power
returns and intention guides me to effective action. *Al*
Killeen's insight and coaching are truly life-savers!

—Greg Osborne
Husband/Father/Entrepreneur

*The "practice" of Level Four living has improved my life on all fronts. **I feel as though I am my most authentic Self in all conditions; that I can go through really rough patches of life and still hang onto my dignity; and most of all, I have more pure and simple joy than I have ever previously experienced.** It allows me to enjoy and truly engage with more people and situations (that at one time I may have avoided), and also to genuinely delight in the friendship and community of "Me, Myself, and I" !! I have a milestone birthday coming up soon, and I can honestly say I have never felt better, both inside and out. I just wish it hadn't taken me this long.*

—Kitty George
Mother/Philanthropist/Consultant

*Al has been a great support to me in attaining and maintaining my "Level 4" (as he calls it) consciousness. At the risk of sounding a bit "woo woo", **the greatest impact that operating in concert with my calling (at Level 4) has is that when I make my mind up to accomplish something, the world seems to bring the people, events and even the resources needed to fulfill on my commitment.** As the 18th Century German Author Goethe said, "the moment one definitely commits oneself then Providence moves too. All sorts of things occur to help one that would never otherwise have occurred."*

—Brad Zimmerman
Husband/Father/Business Owner/Trainer/Coach

Learning and being aware of the need to live at "level-4" resonates in my heart. It requires that I view people thorough a prism of compassion. That I live daily in gratitude and react to obstacles with determination to do what is right, not what is best for me or what feeds my ego.

It encourages me to work towards realizing my goal in life; that of becoming more Holy in a very broken and unholy world. I owe a debt of gratitude to my friend and mentor Al for this enlightenment.

—Ben Zitting
Husband/Father/Top 1% Mortgage Lender

Once you discover how to apply your core values to your decision making, things change. Living, or attempting to live a Level 4 life, seems to clarify choices that lead to discovering and getting what you truly desire. Level 4 living is a way to offset the "humanness" that we all struggle with. Using values as a filter for my life has helped me to create success, happiness, and perhaps even some significance, although I feel my work is not finished.

—Martin Smith, MA MFT
Husband/Father/Therapist/Integrative Mastery Programs Trainer

Giving away my power to fuel others in their times of powerlessness is my one true path to peace. Al's concepts, including that of living a life of Level 4 existence, resonate with and have encouraged me on my path of lawyering with strength and compassion. **May you find what you are missing in the pages of this book**. *Thank you, Al, for your influence, friendship and water cooler conversation.*

—Patricia Bellac
Lawyer/Advocate/Servant/
Adventurer/Wife/Mother

Living at Level 4 has transformed my relationship with family in ways people can only dream about. **To see my children speak from their Level 4 selves is undoubtedly** *the most rewarding treasure in my life. I now know what it means to leave a legacy.*

—Max Yeater
CEO/Husband/Father

*Over the last 17+ years, I have been on a journey of enlightenment with Al Killeen. Along the way I have found my 4th Level of Identity, which has enabled me to share love and understanding with the world. **It has been an amazing gift** and I'm grateful for all of Al's coaching along the way.*

—Dave Williams
Husband/Father/Sales Executive

*Not living a "Level 4" life was a void I felt from within but did not have the tools or awareness to identify. **Through recognizing the personal vision by which I want to exist, I am equipped with a new filter to view life.** The desire to serve something greater than myself has enriched my relationship with God, my family, and the fulfillment of my career.*

—Adam Fleming
Husband/Father/Business Owner

*It's an epidemic. Lives spent on a hamster wheel of pursuits, most often aimed at making ourselves "someone" or acquiring "something." I know that path of spinning futility all too well. It can lead to many destinations, but it will not lead to "significance"… and the fullness and joy it provides. **Al Killeen has captured with crystal clarity the foundational principles which we were created to live out.** In doing so, we awaken to a purposeful life which reflects the best of what it means to be alive. Al's work and life are a gift that* *you should rush to open, and a blessing that will positively change your life for the better. Get off the wheel.... It's time to start living.*

—John Harding
Business Owner/Seeker/Servant

*My life in Level 4 is a softer, kinder, gentler way of living that **allows me to experience happiness personally, professionally and spiritually**. Thank you!*

—Pam Carrington
Mother/Wife/Team Member

Living in Level 4 allows my values to guide me, and my intuition to teach me. I consistently experience happiness, inner peace, and fulfillment since becoming aware of Level 3 and 4 identity. My purpose is to bring out the best in others. I have a smile for everyone. We all have equal light within us to share. I am thankful for my life and the opportunities the universe continually provides. I don't believe in coincidence, rather that every encounter has a purpose.

*I am aware of Level 4 Identity because of Al. He is a portal to its truth. In Level 4, we are all one, and the beautiful emotions of compassion, kindness and love fill the most space in our heart and mind. **Our most important task is to seek to reach our potential, being true to our Self and kind to others along the way.***

In Level 4, you learn to let go of the outcome and live in the moment. Suffering is only in the worry of the future or the regret of the past. Being present and thankful for THIS moment is to live fully.

—Holly Morphew
Entrepreneur/International Speaker/
Business Owner/Financial Expert

I had overcome much in my life to achieve the level of success that I have reached.

However, Al's teachings on being a Level 4 person have helped me to understand that there is more to being fulfilled than just achievement.

The Level 4 person finds fulfillment in the achievement and success of others.

Thank you for your vision and teaching me there is a higher level of living.

—Tina Krupar
Grateful Wife and Mortgage
Lender-Manager/Warrior/Giver

*As you read this book and ponder its precepts, Al will invite you to connect with your 4th Level of Identity. **As you accept this invitation, you will enter a pathway of discovery that transcends Self and will allow you to become the light, the love, the hope, the peace that the purest place of your soul desires.** In so doing, your contribution to those you love and have an opportunity to influence will be magnified indefinitely. Thank you for this invitation, Al, and for the perpetual reminder of who I really am.*

—Timothy Peterson
Husband/Father/Senior Executive/Warrior of Light

Thank you Al Killeen for bringing to the world Soul Proprietorship *and now your new book,* Soul Experience: The 4th Level of Identity. *Through our journey together over the last 17 years, your coaching, friendship and guidance has given me the gift of a Level 4 Identity. It is a gift of real authenticity, living and operating in a space of internal peace and spiritual identity in all areas of my life: Faith, family, friendship, community and profession. Awareness of being in Level 4 awakens me to bring the very best of myself to every situation. It is enlightenment, joy and love.* ***It is a reflection of your true value-based soul. Integrative Mastery and Level 4 Self Awareness has enriched my life beyond measurement and I am forever thankful to you, Al Killeen, for being in my life.***

—Jim Hunter
Husband/Father/Senior Division V.P.

Al Killeen's "Level 4" awakening has been transformative in all facets of my life. It has provided valuable insight to help me develop "Self actualization" beyond ego driven tendencies. This tool not only helps develop professional interactions, but also is a fundamental building block to personal/family vision. Al introduced the concept many years ago and has helped me to develop a natural state of being that operates from the perspective of my "Level 4" Self.

The "4th Level" of identity will lay the groundwork of health & prosperity for many generations to come in both my family and any others that have the Courage to adopt this model of self-guidance.

—Joel Horn
Husband/Father/Business Owner-CEO

I'm genuinely blessed to have Al in my life. His insight, wisdom, and guidance have truly allowed me to transcend at times to the ever elusive Level 4 empowerment, in an otherwise chaotic, confused, and anxiety-filled world. I *would encourage everyone to be open to his words, as **the path to peace, clarity, and a higher level of awareness is all within us. It's in our soul.***

—Cody Hart
Husband/Father/Regional Finance Executive

*While Level 4 looks different for each and every one of us, the pathway that Al Killeen and the Integrative Mastery Program **sets forth and provides anyone who is willing, the opportunity to define and truly understand what our individual higher purpose(s) can be in this world.***

With the development of a personal life vision you are able to more clearly comprehend what your personal Level 4 looks like and when achieved, how it can positively impact you, as well your family, friends, co-workers, clients, and everyone you are blessed to come into contact with.

While sustaining Level 4 is an unrealistic expectation for any earthly being, knowing it exists and working to continually strive for Level 4 allows us to occasionally experience it for both short periods and sometimes extended durations of enhanced consciousness, fulfillment, and peace in knowing all is as it should be. This is sometimes referred to as being in "flow" and that is exactly where and when amazing things happen in our lives, families, and businesses. Brother Al, I want to thank you for helping me to identify my Level 4 through a personal life vision and coaching me over the last few years to more frequently experience the "flow." I am definitely enjoying the ride!

—Eric Amhaus
Husband/Father/Business Owner-Partner

I almost missed meeting Al Killeen in the summer of 2014 as I was teetering on not attending a meeting where he was presenting. As Al presented that morning, I knew within a few moments that a spiritual influence had stepped into my subconscious on why I was not to miss the Integrative Mastery Programs presentation that day. The daily journey from here to eternity that began with Al's presentation has continued to be enhanced over the past 3 years.

Through the Level 4 experience I learned from Al. My relationships are enriched with my wife, family and others I meet in the walk of life. The awareness and practice of Level 4 Identity beyond the daily grind of an ego-based existence helps bring recognition, awareness and mindfulness to my relationships with everyone; that life can be simple, peaceful and purposeful when present in the moments of every day.

So profoundly did I see the power of a Level 4 existence and training, I introduced Integrative Mastery Programs to my business partners so they, too, could have the opportunity to enrich their lives. Further, now our company incorporates this Level 4 cultural values program into our company training.

—Paul Duncan
Husband/Father/CEO

Printed in the USA
CPSIA information can be obtained
at www.ICGtesting.com
LVHW040349150424
777426LV00016B/104